Book Three in the
*On a Wing and a Prayer series*

# Climbing the Heights

*Never before published true and inspirational bird stories!*

*Linda Franklin*

**TEACH Services, Inc.**
PUBLISHING
www.TEACHServices.com • (800) 367-1844

World rights reserved. This book or any portion thereof may not be copied or reproduced in any form or manner whatsoever, except as provided by law, without the written permission of the publisher, except by a reviewer who may quote brief passages in a review.

The author assumes full responsibility for the accuracy of all facts and quotations as cited in this book. The opinions expressed in this book are the author's personal views and interpretations, and do not necessarily reflect those of the publisher.

This book is provided with the understanding that the publisher is not engaged in giving spiritual, legal, medical, or other professional advice. If authoritative advice is needed, the reader should seek the counsel of a competent professional.

Copyright © 2019 Linda Franklin
Copyright © 2019 TEACH Services, Inc.
ISBN-13: 978-1-4796-0942-0 (Paperback)
ISBN-13: 978-1-4796-0943-7 (ePub)
Library of Congress Control Number: 2018913157

Never before published true and inspirational bird stories!

Edited by Linda Marie Harrington Steinke.

Scriptures are taken from the King James Version of the Bible. Public domain.

Illustrated by Duncan Long.

Published by

www.TEACHServices.com • (800) 367-1844

# Other books by Linda Franklin

**On a Wing and a Prayer series**

Book One: *Just a Little Higher*—Comfort comes on soft little wings just when these women need it most!

Book Two: *Staying Aloft*—True stories about men and the extraordinary birds who loved them.

Book Four: *Such Sweet Songs*—Listen carefully! The song of a bird can heal a wounded heart!

**Rainbow series**

Book One: *Rainbow in the Flames*—A tragic fire, a bow of promise, a love of the lasting kind. The healing journey of an optimistic burn survivor (color photos).

Book Two: *Shadows Point to Rainbows*—The remarkable journey of a devoted dog and his beloved boy.

Book Three: *Johnny Sundown*—A wild trapper discovers solace in Canada's Peace Country.

**Survival series**

Book One: *Country in My Heart*—Success stories of people who prayed for a country home. Compiled and edited by Jere and Linda Franklin (b/w photos).

# Dedication

To my husband,

# Jere Franklin

*the first man I ever knew who* really *loved birds!*

# Contents

*To the Reader*—Linda Franklin . . . . . . . . . . . . . . . . . . . . . *vii*

*Introduction* . . . . . . . . . . . . . . . . . . . . . . . . . . . . . . . . *ix*

## Stories

The Chickadee. . . . . . . . . . . . . . . . . . . . . . . . . . . . . . .12

Houdini . . . . . . . . . . . . . . . . . . . . . . . . . . . . . . . . . . .17

Two Little Clowns . . . . . . . . . . . . . . . . . . . . . . . . . . . .24

Roots and Wings . . . . . . . . . . . . . . . . . . . . . . . . . . . . .28

How the Caged Bird Learned to Sing . . . . . . . . . . . . . . .35

Bozo . . . . . . . . . . . . . . . . . . . . . . . . . . . . . . . . . . . . .41

When Stubby Spoke. . . . . . . . . . . . . . . . . . . . . . . . . . .51

Roady, the Road Runner . . . . . . . . . . . . . . . . . . . . . . .62

My Eagle . . . . . . . . . . . . . . . . . . . . . . . . . . . . . . . . . .68

Love Tap . . . . . . . . . . . . . . . . . . . . . . . . . . . . . . . . . .74

Halo . . . . . . . . . . . . . . . . . . . . . . . . . . . . . . . . . . . . .85

Love on the Wild Side—*by Penny Porter* . . . . . . . . . . . . . . .91

## *Poems and Quotes*

In the Hollow of His Hand—*Ray Nichols* . . . . . . . . . . . . . . . . . .16

Weaving Life's Picture—*Anon* . . . . . . . . . . . . . . . . . . . . . . . .23

Today I Smiled—*Unknown* . . . . . . . . . . . . . . . . . . . . . . . . .27

Take to Give—*Ellen White* . . . . . . . . . . . . . . . . . . . . . . . . .34

The Invalid to the Caged Bird—*Martha Lavinia Hoffman (1865–1900)* . .40

Weariness—*Edgar Guest* . . . . . . . . . . . . . . . . . . . . . . . . . .50

My Garden is a Pleasant Place—*Louise Driscoll* . . . . . . . . . . . . .60

Far from the Maddening Crowd—*Nixon Waterman* . . . . . . . . . .67

From the Hand of Love—*Ellen White* . . . . . . . . . . . . . . . . . . .73

Did You Ever Hear an English Sparrow Sing?—*Bertha Johnston* . . . .83

To a Little Girl—*Edgar Guest* . . . . . . . . . . . . . . . . . . . . . . 102

# To the Reader

At an early age, I couldn't resist journaling the splashes of happiness, whispers of wisdom, and even mundane facts that swept across the landscape of my young life. Re-examination helped me decipher the hidden lessons, savor the succulent micronutrients.

At times, re-reading my words left me feeling inspired, inquisitive, hungering for more, and other times I felt hewed, squared and disciplined.

What if I could accurately reproduce a panoramic preview of heavenly beauties and share the sweetness of the clime with others? I bent my efforts to capture object lessons in nature and was heartened by reports that my writings were encouraging a few people.

Then, out of the blue, in flew the birds with their remarkable stories! Before I became privy to their undercover missions, I viewed them merely as blithe spirits, a woodland ornament with ecological work to do. I wonder, now that I have become intimately acquainted with their less recognized work, if their veiled spiritual assignments can be any less essential than their place in nature's subtle balancing act? After hearing story after story from family, friends and acquaintances, I am overwhelmed by incontrovertible evidence that birds are used by God. Close friendship with a bird can open the inner eye to immortal significance in a simple story. There is no thrill like recognizing and capturing the essence of their message to humankind. Birds are sent to sweeten otherwise distasteful character lessons, show us how to care, to connect with each other, and open our eyes to the love and splendor that surround us.

I recognize that I am still recording only faint reflections of glory, but I see a radiance reflected in the eyes of those who share their bird stories with me and then read my interpretation of their experiences.

"God really *did* send me that bird, didn't He, Linda?" I have seen these same people begin to discern and even admit, to worthwhile lessons in trials they had bitterly resented.

The road of life will never be without pebbles and potholes, but, with a little effort, one can see the glories of the sky reflected in any puddle.

Do you dream of having an experience similar to the people in this book? I have a few simple suggestions that might assist you: take time to stop (longer than usual), look (very carefully), listen (with your heart), and envision yourself *Climbing the Heights*.

> *God never leads His children otherwise than they would choose*
> *to be led, if they could see the end from the beginning*
> *and discern the glory of the purpose which they are fulfilling*
> *as co-workers with Him.*
>
> —Ellen White

Linda Franklin<br>
PO Box 840<br>
Chetwynd, BC V0C 1J0<br>
Canada

# Introduction

"Miss Harper, I have been examining your records," said my microbiology professor. "You should be doing much better in my class than you are."

Silence was the only tool in my communication box at the time.

"By missing the first two weeks of class with your illness, you have missed the foundational principles. It will be difficult, but, given your excellent scholastic record, I am sure that you can catch up."

And catch up, I did. In the process, Professor Franklin noticed the inordinate amount of doodles around the edges of my notebook—sketches of microscopic organisms. My pen was my voice and my best friend.

"By request, I am writing a Manual of Medical Mycology," Mr. Franklin revealed at the end of my last tutoring session. "If you would like to work on illustrations for that book, I will be happy to talk to your boss so that you can be assigned to my department four hours a day." By the time that book was printed, we were on a first name basis.

I first realized Jere's fascination with birds during a biology field trip to Malheur Wildlife Refuge in southeastern Oregon. As he patiently taught me the basics of ornithology, his passion for identifying species (by habit, song, and color pattern), his patience in waiting for rare breeds to show themselves, and his reverence for the wilderness spoke volumes to me about his character. I learned to look for wing bars, eye stripes, tail shape and cheek patches. I could soon tell the differences between wrens and kinglets, cranes and herons, blackbirds and cowbirds, warblers and finches. With our trusty field guides, friends and family members, we tramped through miles of Oregon wilderness, disciplining our eyes, ears, and our hearts.

My college graduation brought the conviction that I was now a responsible adult. What would I do to make the world a better place?

Within the next two months I made what I now know to be some significant decisions: 1) I would be a vegetarian, 2) I would be a medical missionary, and 3) I would move to Colorado for my health and for furthering my education. Jere decided to move to Tennessee and study under a pastor he admired.

We both willingly forfeited lucrative positions that offered opportunities for advancement at the laboratory. Then, unexpectedly, after we left the lab closed its doors! We recognized the providential timing of our "sacrifice." During our time in training we chose not to pursue a courtship, but worked hard at becoming who we needed to become, regardless of our mutual attraction. We did not phone or correspond with each other.

By the time we finished our courses, many mutual friends, old and new, advised us that we were right for each other. Even Jere's mentor, W. D. Frazee, recognized providences in our complimentary callings. Under the tutelage of a beloved physician friend, R. B. Moore, my health miraculously improved, so we felt called to add a marriage certificate to our collection of degrees. Elder Frazee performed our wedding and signed our marriage certificate.

Then, causing great consternation among those who knew us, we once more took the road less traveled. We decided to make our home in the country—not just any country—Canada's far north!

There were plenty of practical crises that first year, most of them in the winter months (who would guess that legs would break off of wool long johns drying outside at 40 below?). It was a new challenge just to keep warm without electricity in our little wilderness cabin. Our steep learning curve leveled out a little by the second winter. And then came

*Introduction*

the students—pitching tents, constructing log cabins—helping to build a wilderness school patterned after Jere's dream of encouraging teens the way he, as a rebellious fifteen-year-old, had been helped by one special teacher.

It was on a compulsory camping trip, with three other troublemakers, that Jere first learned about trees, lakes, mountains…and birds.

Knowing Jere has changed my life for the better. He helped me learn to listen so carefully to the birds that I began to hear them with my heart, and that has helped me capture the incredible stories you are about to read.

# The Chickadee

*Who hath measured the waters in the hollow of his hand,
and meted out heaven with the span,
and comprehended the dust of the earth in a measure,
and weighed the mountains in scales, and the hills in a balance?*

—Isaiah 40:12

*I* was in a hurry. I had a big list of duties yet to accomplish. After answering office e-mail, transferring messages to and from my traveling family, bringing in a few armloads of wood and several other chores compulsory to country living, I was definitely running late for my town trip. Nevertheless, I was impressed to kneel and say a special prayer before I left home. As I arose, a name etched itself upon my mind; the name of someone I knew well, but whose personality I found a bit…challenging. Correspondence between us was a distant memory. It occurred to me to send her that beautiful "Footprints" card I'd been saving…

I run up the stairs, two at a time, shuffle through my dwindling supply of greeting cards, address the envelope, rush back downstairs, pull on my winter boots and coat, then go out to start the pickup so it will be warm by the time I finish my note. It is well below zero and there is over a foot of fresh snow on the ground. A kindly neighbor has plowed the driveway, and thankfully, the truck starts.

## The Chickadee

Back in the house, I grab a pen and blow on my hands as I wait for words; something inspiring, but not heavy. Glancing out the dining room window at the bird feeder that my husband, Jere, asked me to maintain in his absence, I see several chickadees patiently taking turns at the last porthole of the nearly empty feeding tube. *Focus, Linda, fill the tube later.*

My friend's childhood was filled with put-downs and physical abuse due to her father's violent temper. My heart hurts for her unstable childhood. I am formulating a sentence to assure her that God knows about her trials. "He's holding you in the hollow of His hand..." I am writing when...

"Crack!" Something hits the window—hard. Having heard that sound before, I drop my pen and open the door expecting to scoop a dead bird off of the porch. Instead, there is a little chickadee, leaning back on its tail, legs sprawled, head wobbling in the rhythmic fashion provoked by dizziness. Picking up the injured bird, I can tell that she is, in all likelihood, a hen, by the circular sweep of her tail having pressed against her nest during the summer months. According to my veterinary friends, the best thing that anyone can do for an injured bird on a cold day is to keep it warm and quiet.

Having raised canaries for several years, and being a lover of anything with feathers, I have held hundreds of birds in various stages of recovery, so it's quite natural for me to gather up the wounded bird, wrap her lightly in a facial tissue, and cup her in my left hand as I attempt to finish the card. I sense that I am not on my own schedule, now. As I finish the sentence I'd started before the bird rescue, about how He is still "holding her in the hollow of His hand..." I smile down at the truth being demonstrated by the little hen snuggling into the hollow of my own hand. Her shiny black eyes are closed, but she is no longer shivering. As I finish the note, I blow gently into her face to assure myself that she is still alive. Her eyes open, but she registers no fear. I slide my finger lightly down her chest and she grips it. With a bird perched on my left hand, a pen in my right, and an object lesson being played out, I recognize a "Kodak moment of the heart" that is mine forever!

As I sign my name, the little hen jumps over to my pen and, though she is still a little shaky, she grips the clip. This is one of those special "connecting times" when I live in a world without time. I make a peeping sound. She turns her head and her shiny black eyes focus on me. They widen with horror when she realizes that she is much too close to a human and flies to a nearby wall hanging.

I net her, walk outside, and slowly turn the net open. She climbs up to the rim and perches there for a few seconds, reorienting herself before she flies to a young aspen beside the woodshed. I watch her from the back porch until I shiver, then I go inside and observe her from the picture window. Within a minute, she flies to the bird feeder, picks out a sunflower seed, and returns to her perch on the aspen. She's OK. The end.

Not quite—that was just the first verse, so to speak!

## Second Verse

I seal the envelope, still thinking about the "coincidence" of the illustration and how much I am like that little chickadee. At times, when I hit the wall, I lose my orientation. Sometimes my little two-year-old granddaughter falls down. She reaches up to me, I dust her off, look into her big blue eyes and ask her what happened. She blinks back tears, then, shaking her head (a little like the chickadee), she says in amazement, "I don't *know*!" So I lift her into my arms in the selfsame way my Father cradles me, warming and comforting me until I can refocus.

It's OK to stay in His embrace until your heart is warmer, too, and quietly listen to Him tell you that one day there will be no more sorrow, death, or crying. It's important to remember, then, that we are never alone. He is only a hug away.

All the way to town, fragments of a long-forgotten song nibble at the far edge of my memory. Long ago and far away I heard a tune…what are those words? The chorus, even the verses said something about "the

## The Chickadee

hollow of His hand," how He protects us, lifts us up when things have gone wrong…

My first stop is a visit to a dental hygienist friend to pick up a copy of her newly published CD, a tribute to her late cousin who wrote the title song. The name of the song? It still gives me chickadee bumps to think about it—*In the Hollow of His Hand!*

# In the Hollow of His Hand

In this life beset with toil, in a world that has gone wrong,
When your heart cannot be lifted by the strains of any song,
When the sins of men are growing,
spreading out through all the land,
He will hold you in the hollow of His hand.

Chorus:
In the hollow of His hand He will keep you tonight.
He will hold you when you feel you cannot stand,
When the troubles of this life have made you weary,
He will hold you in the hollow of His hand.

When the tempest 'round you rages and the waters o'er you roll,
When the darkness presses 'round you
with it's weight upon your soul,
When you're looking through the darkness
trying hard to see the land,
He will hold you in the hollow of His hand.

When I've crossed life's stormy ocean and I'm safe forevermore,
With my friends and loved ones 'round me,
standing there upon that shore,
Then someone may come and ask me how I made it to that land—
I was brought here in the hollow of His hand.

—*Ray Nichols*

# Houdini

*Honour thy father and thy mother: that thy days may be long upon the land which the Lord thy God giveth thee."*

—Exodus 20:12

My friend, I'll call her Millie, told me about a little angel that was such a pale, powdery blue color that she mistook him for highway litter. When she reached down to remove the refuse, the parakeet lifted his head and climbed onto her hand. Within the week that little cherub had changed the way Millie thought about life, and, as she told me herself, she was "...never the same again."

It was one of those days that made me thankful to be alive—a clear, quiet, fresh spring morning—so that even my frustration over Dad's ever-advancing Alzheimer's was lifted for awhile. Returning home from an errand in town, I spied some litter on the main drive that leads into our housing development. Trash was so out of place in our well-kept subdivision that I decided to remove it on my way back from our mailbox. Before I passed the bit of refuse, it moved! My curiosity was aroused. I quickly dropped my mail in the postal box a few hundred yards down the drive, circled back, parked, and got out to inspect this phenomenon.

*Climbing the Heights*

What I found as I bent down was not a piece of debris but a powdery blue parakeet—a small bird with a rounded beak and flat face—a sort of bird version of a Persian cat. His chances of survival were doubtful at best. I couldn't just leave him there on the road, but what could I do?

When I squatted down near the bird to consider my options he nervously backed away from me, but didn't fly. I figured his wings were probably clipped, but if they were, how did he get out in the road? Rather than let him continue in his misguided course I decided to try to catch him. He hurried out of reach. I tried a more passive approach. Laying my hand on the pavement, hoping to reduce his fear, I was both startled and relieved when he willingly climbed onto my forearm. It was my first close encounter with a bird.

I slowly wrapped my hand around his body. He nibbled my fingers, but did little harm. What should I do now? I recalled seeing a red plastic milk crate set out beside a neighbor's trash can on my way to the mailbox; maybe that could serve as a temporary cage until I could find the bird's owner. I rang my own doorbell with my elbow; a biting bird in one hand, plastic crate in the other. My husband answered the door with a rather startled look on his face.

"What the...?"

"Later!" I offered as I hurried past. "Gotta set this bird down before I lose a finger!"

I put the "cage" on the dining room table and tossed the bird inside. He immediately climbed out through the handle hole and seemed content to be on the table—outside the cage. I remembered having some millet on hand, so I sprinkled some on the table and he went to work on the seeds as I went to work taping the handles of the milk crate with 3×5 cards to prevent his escape. But he quickly chewed his way through those. When he also escaped my wiring attempt, I suspected that I was fighting a losing battle.

I put out my hand. He climbed up my arm and hopped onto my shoulder where he proceeded to groom himself and chirp contentedly. Since he would not stay in his temporary cage, I walked around the house with him. I passed the mirror. How beautiful he was; that pale, powdery blue breast, with a pure white head. I looked surprisingly comfortable with a bird on my shoulder. I named the little escape artist Houdini. But, no, I would not be keeping him.

The next day, I talked to neighbors and posted ads everywhere: telephone poles, restaurants, laundromats, and grocery stores. I even placed a "lost" ad in the local paper. I received multiple calls, but none of the callers were missing a bird that fit Houdini's description.

When I told the SPCA my story of finding Houdini, they loaned me a nice big cage without asking for a deposit. In fact, they didn't even ask my name! What a gift! Just what I needed to house my little escapee. Wrong! Like magic, in less than a minute Houdini popped open the door and was, once again, flying free.

I tried to add interest to his confinement by placing picturesque branches for him to perch on, fresh water twice a day, and plenty of seeds. My careful attentions were lost to him. So were the wires with which I bound his cage door. He hated being trapped. His favorite place was on my shoulder. He would escape, then come to me and sit on my shoulder for hours as I worked at my computer. He'd groom his feathers or my hair. He would chirp, and sleep. I was Houdini's favorite tree!

One day, I needed a nap and wanted to lie back in the recliner. I put my hand to my shoulder. Houdini obediently climbed onto my hand, enabling me to lean back in the recliner without crushing him. We slept; me in the chair, Houdini on my finger. He, in fact, preferred never to leave me except to eat.

When it was bed time, or if I had to go out for awhile, Houdini seemed to know when I was planning his imprisonment and would fly across the room, or through several rooms, to my husband's shoulder. It was the only time he sought refuge with my husband. He always preferred a shoulder rather than a curtain rod. I would eventually catch and cage him and he would squawk indignantly. I learned to hate the cage, too, because

Houdini got a bad case of depression when he was trapped. I wrapped the cage as tightly as I could in half-inch deer netting; that slowed him down, but too soon he was out again.

I watched with increasing respect as that fiercely independent little creature searched intently for at least ten minutes before he found a weakness in the netting. Twice I wrapped it; twice he struggled against the netting. Inevitably he freed himself and went looking for seeds on the tabletop, more content with his freedom than with the seeds. Even when I wasn't watching, I knew when he had succeeded in escaping because his discontented mutter would change to a triumphant chirp. He would throw out his chest, and chirp until I acknowledged his expertise. Of course, I would place him back in his cage where he would sulk quietly until he came up with another escape plan. If a bird could look sad, he did.

Watching Houdini's ever-deepening depression at being caged clouded my days. I knew what I had to do. I had to find a bird lover who could stand to confine Houdini for his health and safety. While I awaited the right caller, I realized that I would never again appreciate a zoo. However well a cage is camouflaged, it is a poor excuse for freedom.

One morning, with this little blue angel on my shoulder as I read my daily devotional, I was nudged into considering Dad's care:

*It is not best to establish institutions for the care of the aged, that they may be in a company together. Nor should they be sent away from home to receive care. Let the members of every family minister to their own relatives. When this is not possible, the work belongs to the church, and it should be accepted both as a duty and as a privilege. All who have Christ's spirit will regard the feeble and aged with special respect and tenderness. ...Children, let your parents, infirm and unable to care for themselves, find their last days filled with contentment, peace, and love. For Christ's sake let them go down to the grave receiving from you only words of kindness, love, mercy, and forgiveness...*

*Adventist Home,* page 363.

*Houdini*

As I read, I was struck forcibly with the similarity between Dad and Houdini; their spirits fell as their freedoms decreased. It was one of those golden moments of recognition that I could not ignore, and I reaffirmed my vow to do whatever I could to help stretch Dad's sense of freedom. True, he needed close supervision, but, with a little extra effort, maybe I could camouflage his cage. On his good days, I would look for opportunities to let him make some simple choices that might help him feel more independent.

That same day, I received a phone call from a woman whose parakeet was pining because her mate had escaped. I knew, from her description of the missing bird, that it was not Houdini, but when I offered him to her as a replacement, the woman was interested. I asked her to bring a suitable cage ("suitable," in this case, solid metal walls and a sturdy combination lock).

She came early that same evening with a yellow female parakeet in a large cage. Houdini, perching happily on my shoulder (as usual) chirped loudly, and Miss Sunshine chirped in response. It was love at first sight! Into the cage went Houdini. Voluntarily! They were still snuggling when their mistress took them out to her car.

The house seemed a little too quiet after Houdini left. I tried not to, but I couldn't help wondering about him every time I worked at the computer, sat in my easy chair, or looked in the mirror. Had I really done the best I could for him?

When the phone rang a few days later, I received a favorable report from Houdini's adoptive mother, telling me that the cage was on their enclosed porch, that Houdini was allowed to fly free daily, and always willingly returned to his mate.

"My husband loves him!" She laughed. "Houdini thinks Bill is his own personal tree!"

I couldn't stop smiling; my little escape artist, had found an understanding home. There really are no "coincidences" in life, are there?

*Climbing the Heights*

Houdini's new Mom answered my ad at precisely the right moment. Any sooner and my conclusions about Dad's care would have fallen short of the strong conviction to which I now subscribe. I ask for and allow his input whenever possible. It does seem that my new attitude is helping Dad feel less restricted.

Houdini will always hold a special place in my heart. I only had him for a week, but that "little bit o' litter" completely changed how I view age, and a cage. Noble creature, I thank you, and my father thanks you, too.

---
All names in this story are pseudonyms.

# Weaving Life's Picture

My life is but a weaving between my Lord and me;
I may not choose the colors—He knows what they should be.
For He can view the colors upon the upper side
While I can see it only upon this under side

Not 'til the loom is silent and the shuttles cease to fly
Will God unroll the pattern and explain the reason why
The dark threads were as needful in the Weaver's skillful hand
As the threads of gold and silver in the pattern which He planned.

Sometimes He weaveth sorrow, which seemeth strange to me,
But I will trust His judgment and work on faithfully.
'Tis He who fills the shuttle; He knows just what is best.
So I shall trust in earnest, and leave to Him the rest.

At last, when life is ended, with Him I shall abide.
Then I shall view the pattern upon the upper side.
Then I shall know the reason why pain and joy entwined
Were woven in the fabric of the life that God designed.

—*Anon*

# Two Little Clowns

*A merry heart doeth good like a medicine:
but a broken spirit drieth the bones.*

—Proverbs 17:21

*My good friend Piper had been so sick. She knew she had to get her spring cleaning done, but her energy was just not returning. She prayed, but nothing seemed to happen, at least not until the clowns dropped in…literally! It was easy to capture their visit in my imagination because I have been in Piper's house, but I would love to have been there that eventful day.*

"Knock, knock."

Who could that be? I lifted my head from the couch where I had collapsed after finishing the breakfast dishes and offering up a listless petition for strength.

*Lord, please help me get well.*

I knew that my husband, Stanley, was worried about me. He had tested my smile as he ate his breakfast, but it still wasn't working. Everything that should have seemed humorous was no longer the least bit amusing to me. Even a smile took too much effort. I was definitely not ready for company.

"Knock, knock, knock."

I slowly raised myself to a sitting position, trying to ignore the nauseating dizziness that had been troubling me since my illness began over a month earlier.

"Knock, knock, knock."

I tipped myself forward and strained to look out the window. There were blossoms in the orchard that weren't there yesterday.

*Lord, I should be feeling invigorated by the promise of new life, but I have been sick for so long! Will I ever be well again?*

"Knock, knock, knock, knock."

*Lord, I need rest. Must I open to this visitor?*

When I finally staggered to my feet, I realized that the knocking was not coming from the front door where our guests usually arrive, but from inside the wood stove! Stanley had not built a fire because the past days had been unseasonably warm. I stepped closer to the stove.

"Knock, knock."

Cautiously I opened the stove door. There, huddled together in the ashes, sat two very sooty fledglings. As light entered their abode, they turned toward me and blinked. So did I.

"Well, where did you come from?" I asked. Looking back at each other, they appeared to be wondering the same thing. I reached in and picked up one of the youngsters. He was absolutely unafraid. I shuffled to the front door, blew off his sooty feathers and placed him on the porch rail. The second sibling appeared to be awaiting my return. I cleaned him off and placed him beside the first fledgling. Snuggling together comfortably, they looked up at me, almost as if they were smiling. In the morning sun they appeared to be dark brown. I could not tell what kind of birds they would become, but as I watched them flutter away together with the comical unsteady wings so characteristic of a first-flight, I thought I felt a smile tugging at one corner of my mouth.

"Thank You for my visitors," I muttered as I followed a sunbeam back to my couch. In less than an hour, I was awakened.

"Knock, knock, knock."

*Climbing the Heights*

Again? I shuffled toward the stove. This time the two fledglings were sitting side by side in the ashes already looking upward expectantly when I opened the door. I picked them both up, and spoke to them as we walked together to the front porch where I once more blew the ashes from their feathers.

"The chimney is not a safe place to practice your landings," I grinned. "You'd best stay in the trees, little ones."

They flew across the yard, their flight pattern a little steadier. Once again I returned to my sunbeam and closed my eyes. But my ears wouldn't sleep; they seemed to be listening without my permission. Sure enough, the sound came again in just a matter of minutes this time.

"Knock, knock."

Interestingly, I no longer considered this rescue operation an interruption. I walked purposefully to the stove and opened the door. This time I could swear they were smiling up at me. I smiled back. It didn't take any effort at all.

"You funny little clowns!" I giggled. "Why are you doing this?"

Once more they flew away toward the orchard. Once more I returned to my sunbeam. Feeling a little more energetic, I decided to remain sitting upright. As I picked up my Bible, the sun fell across the pages as I slowly leafed through my favorite Psalms and Proverbs. Reading aloud, the words and sunshine miraculously recharged me.

"Knock, knock, knock."

Laying aside my favorite Book, and anticipating the arrival of my two little clowns, I walked briskly back to the stove. It was giving me a sense of accomplishment to be able to re-rescue the chicks. By nightfall I had rescued them ten times!

Or...had *they* rescued *me*?

On my last trip to the front porch I held one in each hand so that we were eye to eye and said, "Thank you!"

Away they flew, much more sure of themselves, now. Apparently their assignment was accomplished. They never returned.

For the first time in weeks, I had a smile for Stanley when he returned home.

## Today I Smiled

Today I smiled, and all at once things didn't look so bad.
Today I shared with someone else, a bit of hope I had.

Today I sang a little song, and felt my heart grow light,
And walked a happy little mile, with not a cloud in sight.

Today I worked with what I had and longed for nothing more,
And what had seemed like only weeds, were flowers at my door.

Today I loved a little more, complained a little less,
And in the giving of myself, forgot my weariness.

*—Unknown*

# Roots and Wings

*Cast thy bread upon the waters:*
*for thou shalt find it after many days.*

—Ecclesiastes 11:1

*I* don't know of anyone who loves birds and blossoms more than my friend Linda, except maybe me! When she suffered the loss of her husband, Dave, we became closer friends. She had some of my canaries in her sun room where she also kept a profusion of houseplants—her sanctuary. I still have the beautiful willow rocking chair and daybed in my prayer garden that her teenage son, Zach, bartered with me to provide his mother the usual plethora of pastel flowers for her window boxes, hanging baskets, patio pots, and gardens when her disability* increased. Linda's most unique parenting influence was her love of beauty; can a mother do better for her children than teach them to seek object lessons among their country surroundings? She felt she possessed far less than half of the parenting skills that her sons needed, but her rescue of the little flycatchers demonstrates great parental depth perception—the essence of roots and wings.

Just getting dressed felt like an Olympic event that day. Household chores that had once been such a joy to me had become insurmountable challenges. Breathing had become painful after my exposure to a toxic dump in our driveway had severely compromised my lungs. My sons, Zach and Josh, had suffered strange symptoms, too, but they were finally able to attend school, and had just left for the day. I was sitting at the kitchen table sipping the last of my Red Zinger tea, wondering where I would find the strength for the day's tasks when the phone rang.

"Good morning, Linda," said a cheerful voice. "My husband found a nest of four chicks in a culvert he had to remove yesterday. Of course, my first thought was of you! You are so good at rescuing orphans, especially chicks! Since it was late when my husband got home, I kept the chicks overnight, but I really haven't a clue how to care for them, and they are very inactive this morning."

"Bring them over," I invited. "I'll do my best."

*Father, have I said the right thing? What else could I do? All of my life, it has come natural to me to care for the wounded creatures of Your creation. Did You send me that gift? I re-surrender my talents to You, Lord. Help me make a success of this call for help, for Thy sake.*

## Within Reach

When the chicks arrived, my heart sank. "Inactive" was an understatement; they were cold, weak, and didn't even have feathers yet. What was their parentage? What kind of food did they need? As I sat in silence, watching the seemingly lifeless chicks and waiting for a plan to emerge, I heard some flies buzzing in the window.

"Once again, with a little effort, what I need is within reach," I mumbled, smiling to myself in spite of my exhaustion. As I collected the chicks' breakfast, I benefited, once more, from my Father's timely provision. "When I exhaust my strength and resources, He supplies my needs." My boys and I didn't dwell in luxury, but we'd never gone hungry after their father died. I brushed away my tears, determined to re-direct my outlook.

I held the first fly above the nest. To my surprise and delight, four little beaks opened wide! Those scrawny necks could barely support the little heads that wobbled back and forth with the strain, but they ate. There was a fly for each one.

*Climbing the Heights*

When Josh and Zach came home from school, they fell in love with the chicks and immediately assigned themselves as providers. With great enthusiasm, they combed the lawn, garden and forest for bugs and worms surrounding the simple log cabin that Dave had built. I loved living where we could see the handiwork of the Great Designer. Sure, we were reminded often enough—by evidence of fang and claw—that this world was not our home. But, if life was perfect, what need would we have of heaven?

Preparing the grasshoppers that the boys brought was a repulsive task, but they were easily caught and the chicks loved them. Thinking to save my boys time and effort, I obtained some "fishing worms" from a local hardware store. When I started to open the worm container, I just couldn't do it. I shivered and looked up helplessly at my boys.

"I'm sorry, but I absolutely cannot handle worms," I said.

"I'll do it, Mom," said Josh. While I looked the other way, he removed a worm from the container. He actually couldn't accomplish the task either, but I didn't know that until after I had left the kitchen and taken the worm container outside. Not wanting Josh to do something that I could not accomplish, I decided to release the rest of the worms in my garden. When I dumped the worms out, I couldn't believe the *size* of the night crawlers that were hiding there! They were over a foot long! They looked like snakes! I don't even know how they had been able to keep themselves covered with dirt! Suddenly I had a terrible thought: if these monster worms multiplied, my own garden would be off limits! Little worms were bad enough, but what could I do, now? Those worm-snakes were scurrying away at a rapid rate!

Fortunately, my neighbor dropped by just as I was considering the situation (panic would more accurately describe what I was feeling at the time). She quickly gathered up the worms and replaced them in their container while I stood by, paralyzed with fear.

"Where did you get these huge night crawlers?" she asked.

I couldn't answer her for awhile, but she soon had me laughing at myself. Seems to me that she gave them to a fisherman, and I was happy to be rid of them.

The chicks spent their nights in a tissue-lined shoe box beside my bed. I fed them whenever I heard them stir. It was a challenge to add this interruption to my sleep-deprived nights, but I couldn't let the babies die without giving it the good old-fashioned try!

And those little chicks thrived! Not only were they gobbling grasshoppers at an incredible rate, they had learned to appreciate a formula I had invented for my canary and finch nestlings: mashed hard boiled egg, bread crumbs, powdered bird vitamins from the pet store, with a sprinkle of water to moisten the mix. The unidentified chicks grew rapidly and soon feathered out in the familiar pattern of a flycatcher. The boys outfitted their large cage with fresh aspen branches, and they were soon ready for their first flying lesson.

## Flying Free

The three us knew that we couldn't keep our little orphans forever, but when Josh and Zach took the chicks outside it turned out to be a highly memorable event for me that even today remains close to my heart. Only those who have experienced a long-awaited warm spring day in the foothills of the northern Canadian Rockies can begin to sense the true splendor of the pungent, healing scent of cottonwood, the balmy sunshine streaming through the tall pines, and the promise of a harvest to come from the tiny green shoots in my newly planted garden.

This was one of those days destined to stay in my heart forever. That day, I clearly saw the black and white of motherhood. The purpose of our care for these baby birds was that they might fulfill the purpose of their birth. Proper nurturing results in growth; growth results in maturation; maturation brings with it the desire for exploration. I knew the sequence, but my heart wasn't quite ready to let go. Their departure seemed premature. Is the human heart ever in step with divine timing?

Solomon says, *to everything there is a season; a time to weep and a time to laugh.* It takes the welcomed and the unwelcomed events to complete the picture of life, just as surely as it takes both sun and rain to make a rainbow.

As much as I would love to see a rainbow every day, I couldn't necessarily welcome a daily drenching. As I watched those little chicks testing their wings, their training seemed to foreshadow what I would eventually face. Too soon, my own young fledglings would be scanning the far horizons, eager to test their wings. That thought was about as welcomed as a nightcrawler in my bed! With an intense pang of responsibility, I vowed to do all within my power to deepen their roots and strengthen their hearts that they might direct their flight toward the right goals in life.

*There is a God above, and the light and glory from His throne rests upon the faithful mother as she tries to educate her children to resist the influence of evil. No other work can equal hers in importance. She has not, like the artist, to paint a form of beauty upon canvas, nor, like the sculptor, to chisel it from marble. She has not, like the author, to embody a noble thought in words of power, nor, like the musician, to express a beautiful sentiment in melody. It is hers, with the help of God, to develop in a human soul the likeness of the divine* (Ministry of Healing, Ellen White, page 377).

Our chicks spent one last night in their cage. Josh set it on our front porch the next morning and opened the door. The chicks were out in no time. They circled the house twice and then they were gone. So quickly! It was as if the entire earth held a moment of silence; a time of loss, like a sort of funeral dirge, for which I had tried to prepare myself in vain. Was the earth a little richer for our efforts with these four adorable young birds? I prayed it was, but I felt so empty. I watched and waited, but they did not return. I wanted to feel elation, but I was disappointed.

## A Glimpse of Glory

On a dismal day that autumn, a particularly difficult morning, I sat on the couch in my sun room—the special corner that Dave had built for my art creations, where I could nurture my houseplants and listen to my canaries sing. Because my illness had progressed to where I could no longer create oil paintings because of my newly-acquired sensitivities to chemical fumes, I sat dejectedly thinking about the pictures I would never paint. Death and illness had dulled my joy, and life had taken on some dark tones that I had rarely painted. I was now on oxygen full time, dependent on others for all but my most personal needs. I'd even limited the number of birds in my care because I had so little strength. Winter would soon be here, and there was nothing sweet about that thought, either. For over an hour, my gloomy storm cloud obliterated the rainbow of God's sustaining power. I cried in despair.

*Father God, I just don't see how I can go on. I have nothing left! Medical science has no explanation for my illness. They say I can't get well. I can't even take care of myself, let alone my boys. And here comes winter...*

It wasn't really a prayer, it was a whine of self-pity. Would God answer that kind of a plea? I am here to tell you that He did! When I opened my eyes, there on the window sill, looking back at me was one of my olive-sided flycatcher chicks! He was mature, now—no doubt on his way south for the winter—just dropping by to say "thanks." If ever a bird could smile, he did!

I smiled back through my tears. What a gentle and timely token! When I felt completely grounded, unable to flutter, He made His presence known, reminding me that even my little faith, the weight of one little chick feather, is enough to lift my spirit when I stay grounded in Him.

"Strengthen your roots," my heart heard, "Together we can fly up and over the mountains that are pressing in on you. Faith is enough."

*Oh, thank You, Father! You are with me. You comfort me. Even in this vale of shadows, You shine on me. You send me little gifts, like birds that I can help. Thank you for giving me "a measure of faith", if only the weight of a feather.*

---

(*Linda's story *"Rainbow in the Dark"* is in Book One of this series, *"Just a Little Higher"*)

# Take to Give

*All things both in heaven and in earth declare
that the great law of life is a law of service.
The infinite Father ministers to the life of every living thing.
Christ came to the earth "as He that serveth." Luke 22:27.*

The same law of service is written upon all things in nature.
The birds of the air, the beasts of the field, the trees of the forest,
the leaves, the grass, and the flowers, the sun in the heavens
and the stars of light—all have their ministry.
Lake and ocean, river and water spring—each takes to give.

*—Ellen White*

# How the Caged Bird Learned to Sing

*Ye shall have a song, as in the night when a holy solemnity is kept;
and gladness of heart, as when one goeth with a pipe
to come into the mountain of the Lord, to the mighty One of Israel.*

—Isaiah 30:29

Stan and Piper have been our close friends for many years, often playing special music for us when we present seminars in the eastern US. When we heard of Piper's illness in October, we began praying earnestly for them. Now it was March, and having received a "progress report" that was not good news, we felt the need to support and uplift them. Guess who received the encouragement when we phoned them?

Piper answered the phone with a voice that successfully camouflaged her suffering, though we had received word that she was in pain. We asked her about everyday challenges first, getting a feel for her coping skills. After assuring us that their needs were being met in wonderful ways, Piper wanted to talk about what really mattered.

"I feel so blessed," she said with enthusiasm, "God has given me much joy. The last few mornings, my quiet time with Him has been so sweet. I feel so much closer, as if I have had an awakening to God's true goodness. I *know* He will see us through. I have received the assurance that Stanley and I have nothing to worry about."

"We feel your prayers, Jere!" Stan exclaimed. "It is so obvious to us that the Lord is caring for our every need. We are in a nice basement suite at my folks' place. It is wheelchair accessible, which our country home in West Virginia is not, and we have discovered that Tennessee offers complete insurance coverage to residents with Piper's illness. What a blessing that is!"

"I was going to be nosey and ask about your finances, Stan," Jere said. "I know you have quit your job to care for Piper."

"Well, I've been given a cup that I don't want to swallow, Jere," Stan answered gravely. "But one friend recently shared a couple of quotes that are helping me face the challenge."

*"Oh for a living active faith! We need it; we must have it, or we shall faint and fail in the day of trial. The darkness that will then rest upon our path must not discourage us or drive us to despair. It is the veil with which God covers his glory when He comes to impart rich blessings"* (*Ministry of Healing*, by E. White).

*"Above the distractions of the earth He sits enthroned; all things are open to His divine survey; and from His great and calm eternity He orders that which His providence sees best. God does not propose to be called to account for His ways and works. It is for His glory to conceal His purposes now; but by and by they will be revealed in their true importance. But He has not concealed His great love, which lies at the foundation of all His dealings with His children"* (*Faith I Live By*, by E. White).

"Jere, if I had the power to heal Piper, I would do it in a heartbeat," Stan explained. "But I have the sweet assurance that God is looking down from His perfect Eternity, seeing a reality that I can't see. If Piper and I are separated, it won't be for long, though it is a reality I would choose not to experience."

Jere found it difficult to answer. I was listening in on the conversation, unable to trust my voice either. From Piper's recent e-mail, I had learned that she had written a song about "The Caged Bird" and I wanted to hear it. I took a deep breath, tried to relax my throat, and prepared to ask my question.

"Hi, Piper," I said, "I'm eager to know the words to the song you mentioned in your e-mail about "The Caged Bird."

"If you like, Stanley and I can sing it to you," she offered. Then, almost instantly she burst forth into song, like the canary that simply has too much praise to contain. She must have had her guitar already in her lap.

I was amazed at the strength of her voice; Stanley usually has to decrease his volume because Piper's voice is naturally much softer than his. Not this evening; Piper sang as if she had a microphone! They sang, their harmony exact, synchronized, and ringing with a depth of conviction such as we had never heard before. What a thrill to hear soul mates, locked together in a sacred triangle with God's will foremost, focused beyond the grave that lay open before them. The song was definitely a miracle melody.

It was difficult to speak past the lump that was left in my throat as Piper strummed the last chords I would ever hear her play. "That was so beautiful Piper. Please e-mail me those words! What a powerful message." Here is her reply:

Dear Jere and Linda,
It was truly a blessing to speak with you both as well. You both are very near and dear to our hearts and we have enjoyed every opportunity we have had to be with you.
Here are the words for my gift of song from Jesus:

## The Caged Bird

*In the fullest light of the day,*
*Hearing music of other voices*
*The caged bird will not sing the song*
*The master seeks to teach her.*
*She learns a trill of this and that*
*But never a whole melody.*
*So the master gently works his plan;*
*He simply covers the cage.*

*Climbing the Heights*

*Chorus:*
*He has a song to teach us*
*In shadows of affliction;*
*And when we have learned it*
*We will sing it forever more.*

*In a place where the bird can only hear*
*The one song she is to sing,*
*In darkness she tries many times*
*To sing the song 'til it's learned.*
*She then breaks out in melody,*
*The master uncovers the cage,*
*And brings her forth in the light to sing.*
*So God deals with His children.*

*Chorus:*
*He has a song to teach us*
*In shadows of affliction*
*And when we have learned it—*
*We will sing it forevermore;*
*We will sing it forevermore!*
*Praise the Lord!*

I feel so honored and blessed that He bestowed this gift to me. It reflects my experience completely and now that I'm so experiencing that song, all I can do is share. He has filled my cup to overflowing. I almost can't contain myself sometimes. I love Him so very much and will spend the rest of my days, life, and breath praising Him!

May you have a blessed day.

Love, Piper

*How the Caged Bird Learned to Sing*

Piper was inspired to write her song from *Ministry of Healing*, page 472–473, by Ellen White. The passage goes on to explain:

"Let us remember that while the work we have to do may not be our choice, it is to be accepted as God's choice for us. Whether pleasing or unpleasing, we are to do the duty that lies nearest. ...He has reasons for sending us to the place toward which our feet have been directed. ...Our plans are not always God's plans. He may see that it is best for us and for His cause to refuse our very best intentions, as He did in the case of David. But of one thing we may be assured, He will bless and use in the advancement of His cause those who sincerely devote themselves and all they have to His glory. If He sees it best not to grant their desires He will counterbalance the refusal by giving them tokens of His love and entrusting to them another service. ...We are never called upon to make a real sacrifice for God. Many things He asks us to yield to Him, but in doing this we are but giving up that which hinders us in the heavenward way. Even when called upon to surrender those things which in themselves are good, we may be sure that God is thus working out for us some higher good. ...In the future life the mysteries that here have annoyed and disappointed us will be made plain. We shall see that our seemingly unanswered prayers and disappointed hopes have been among our greatest blessings."

Before the phone call ended that evening, Jere reminded Stan and Piper that our home was open to them if they ever needed it.

"Thanks, Jere," said Stan. "You folks are our adopted parents and your opinion carries a lot of weight with us."

After the call, I sat quietly in the office for several minutes allowing their cheering witness to sink into my soul. Stan and Piper were in the deepest of winters, but they chose to sing. Never have I heard a more eloquent demonstration of hope and truth combined than that evening when, singing to us from the opposite end of North America, Piper radiated the song that illumined her soul during her darkest, brightest hour.

I pray that I have not heard her last chord.

---

**NOTE:** To order Piper's last CD, *The Caged Bird Set Free*, email Stanley Ivins (ivinsimprovements@gmail.com).

# The Invalid to the Caged Bird

What are you singing my beautiful bird?
What are the words of your song?
How can you carol when always denied
The freedom for which you must long?

Once, where the wild roses blushing at morn
Grew pale at the sunset's first glow;
Hidden from sight by a cool, leafy screen,
Your little nest swung to and fro.

There your bright eyes first awoke to the light,
And your restless wings scarcely could wait;
So eager to try in the great outside world,
Their portion of fortune or fate.

But long ere your delicate velvety wings
Were penciled with faint lines of blue;
With the first eager taste of sweet freedom's delight,
A prison stood ready for you.

Have you forgotten the shadowy trees,
With the lily-bells nodding below?
Have you forgotten the rocky hillside,
Where the wood-pinks and buttercups grow?

There I, too, wandered, unfettered and free,
Ere my prison doors hid them from sight;
I too, am longing to see them again
Aglow in the sun's golden light.

For I am a prisoner, too, beautiful bird,
Shut in from the beauties I love.
Shut in from the blossoms and verdure beneath,
And the blue of the cloud-lands above.

O teach me, sweet singer, your pure, artful song,
That I may your happiness share;
And forget in the joy of a rapture like them,
The phantoms of hope and despair!

—*Martha Lavinia Hoffman (1865–1900)*

# Bozo

*Whosoever shall give to drink unto one of these little ones
a cup of cold water only in the name of a disciple,
verily I say unto you, he shall in no wise lose his reward.*

—Matthew 10:42

*I* met Ginny Allen when she was the guest speaker at our BC Women's Retreat. She personally sought out my friend, Lila, a recovering addict that I had brought to the retreat. Lila had searched for love in some interesting places. Ginny gave her a hug, prayed with her, and pressed a small autographed volume about real love into Lila's hand. Lila wept her appreciation for Ginny's caring concern. That's Ginny's technique; whether listening or speaking, quoting a passage of Scripture or telling a story, she can tug on a heartstring, somewhere in the vicinity of your tear manufacturing headquarters, and leave you feeling cleaner, refreshed, more empowered. She treats wounds, inside and out.

Among Ginny's most memorable accounts that weekend was her story of Bozo, an orphaned starling chick. I am grateful she gave permission to include it in this volume.

If my friend Ginny was a bird, she would be a mother quail, but instead of being followed by a dozen miniature replicas bobbing along behind her, there would be wounded fledglings of every color and description limping along in her wake. She would inspect the ranks at intervals, hovering closest to the wounded, encouraging those who had stumbled, and then, after meeting their physical needs, she'd lead them to The Water for refreshment. How do I know? Because it is those who are hurting most who have always received the most help from Nurse Ginny.

## Nurse with a Passion

Ginny is often preoccupied with thoughts and prayers for her fledglings—mostly teenagers at the large public high school in the western United States where she spent many years as school nurse. Many of Ginny's "orphans" who have no one to truly care for them, drop by her office for a word of encouragement, or a quick hug between classes. It's a tough-looking group; uncultured, hard-hitting ruffians, even gang members who come in for a chat or ask a word of advice unrelated to medicine. They know she loves them—she remembers their name! Her association with the "rabble" is cause for concern among Ginny's close friends and relatives. She can repeat many amusing stories about places she goes where angels might…well, at least think twice.

Ginny and her husband, out with another couple for the evening, had to cross an unlit parking lot in a rough section of a large city. It was daylight when they parked, but it was dark before they returned. Motivated by the horror stories they had heard about the dangerous gangs in that particular neighborhood, the younger couple sprinted across the parking lot. When they reached the other side, breathless from their run, they looked back to see Ginny and her husband far behind them…surrounded by a gang! They were about to dial the police on their cell phone when they heard Ginny laughing! A short little lady was being hugged by a tall, muscular black man, the gang leader, who just "happened" to turn out to be a student Ginny had been counseling, and loving, for the past several months. The permanent laugh-crinkles deepen around Ginny's sparkling brown eyes as she explains her predicament.

"There we were, my husband and I, hurrying across that dark, abandoned parking lot, when we heard someone in the shadows holler out, 'Hey!' Of course we ignored the command, already sensing the danger we were in since we couldn't keep up with the younger couple running ahead of us. In seconds, we found ourselves surrounded by a really mean-looking gang. Then we heard the leader speak authoritatively.

"Hey, don't hassle these two!" my friend Jordan growled. "Ginny's my school nurse! She's my friend!"

## Forgotten Children

Though she has many amusing narratives, some are almost too painful to share. Ginny can't relate the story of Kelli without a catch in her voice. Kelli's adventures on the city streets began the day her father was sentenced to life in prison. When her mother's boyfriend said he couldn't live with Kelli's mother if there were children in the house, her mother pushed little six-year-old Kelli out onto the street. Ginny has heard some pretty ugly stories, in fact, she has a fat file of suicide notes, but she was especially challenged to conceal her horror as Kelli slowly, over a series of days, unfolded her life to Ginny. It was so gruesome that Ginny conferred with a social worker for verification.

"Kelli hasn't even told you half of what she has suffered, Ginny," the social worker assured her. "She has had it rougher than any child we've had in the system." Ginny continued to take time with Kelli and the wounded girl responded to her genuine warmth and concern.

"How did you survive, Kelli?" Ginny asked.

"I ate out of garbage cans and slept under bridges," Kelli said, her eyes reflecting a hardness born of rejection. In order to provide herself a warm bed in which to sleep and a little food in her stomach, Kelli had learned to make her way in the street as a prostitute by age ten and delivered her first child shortly after she turned 12. Her baby girl was taken to live with relatives in the south and Kelli never saw her again. Pregnant again at age 14, she had another little girl who died under suspicious circumstances during an all night card party involving drinking and drugs. Kelli had been put on probation for many reasons: running away from all of her foster homes, drugs, petty theft, drinking and driving, and prostitution. Kelli related her story in matter-of-fact tones, shedding no tears. Ginny's heart was wrenched with every new revelation. When Ginny could think of nothing to say, she would just hug Kelli, hoping to replace a little of the affection she had missed as a fledgling flung from the nest before she was even fully feathered.

Knowing that Ginny's door was always open to her, Kelli began to feel valued. She often dropped by the nurse's office, sometimes just quietly fingering the stray curls at the back of Ginny's neck while "her nurse" caught up on paperwork. Steadily, Kelli's tough exterior softened. Then, one fateful day all of Kelli's new-found confidence seemed to hang in shreds from her thin shoulders as she walked into the office. There was fear in her eyes.

"I have to go to court because of the fire I started," she told Ginny, her lower lip quivering. "If I'm convicted of arson I will have to go to a juvenile detention home until I am 18." Then she began to weep, "Oh, Ginny! I'm so afraid."

Embracing the sobbing girl, Ginny assured her softly, "Well, Honey, I can't change the judge's verdict, but I will go to court with you and I will be there for you whenever you need me."

Just before the hearing, Kelli ran away, and Ginny never saw or heard from her again. She watched closely for the familiar mop of blonde hair wherever she went; she checked beneath bridges, and stopped by several homeless shelters. When she asked a policeman about Kelli's chances of survival, the officer was not encouraging.

"We'll no doubt find her dead in a park during our morning rounds one of these days, Ginny," he said sadly, shaking his head. "Unfortunately, the odds of survival for her type aren't any too good, you know."

Like Kelli, a few of Ginny's children slip from her grasp, but many lives have been changed for the better because of her listening ear, her timely advice, her caring smile, her understanding pat on an arm or back, and a caring hug when desired. That brings us to Bozo's grand entrance!

## Nestling into Her Heart

It was spring break. As Ginny caught up on some housecleaning chores, she was thinking about "her children," saying a prayer for each youngster that paraded through her thoughts. Just as she turned off the vacuum cleaner, the doorbell rang. It was a little neighbor girl, smiling broadly, holding her treasure out to Ginny—a tiny chick with a wide open beak.

"I found thith birdie on the ground, Mitheth Ginny," lisped the child through missing front teeth. "There were cat-th coming, and tho I picked him up. Can you take care of him?" The little girl dumped her bundle into Ginny's hands, then skipped happily away.

Ginny cradled the ugly chick, wondering what to do. Repulsed by the nakedness of the prehistoric-looking creature with the loud mouth, she quickly decided that she would not be getting attached to him, but she could, at least, feed him. She had cared for many orphans: numerous children, and several kinds of animals, but never such a tiny chick!

She settled on an "infant formula" of bread and milk that she thought might work, and soon found herself conversing with the hungry, noisy bird as he gulped down his first of many meals at Ginny's table.

Well, if she was going to carry on a conversation, the bird had to have a name. Because of the bright yellow outline around his beak that reminded her of a clownish smile, Ginny dubbed him "Bozo."

"Life isn't always fair, is it, Bozo?" Ginny intoned softly as he guzzled the moist crumbs from her fingers. "I guess you and I will just have to make do, eh?" By the end of that first feeding Ginny knew, in spite of her resolve, that Bozo had already nestled his way right down into her heart. Wiping his scrawny chest with a small cotton cloth, she placed him in a tissue-lined shoebox and sandwiched the remainder of her spring cleaning around Bozo's feeding schedule.

As busy as she was, the only way Bozo could have the timely encouragement and food he needed throughout the day was to attend school with Nurse Ginny. Secure in his little basket, Ginny not only took him to school, he went shopping, and visiting, too. He even went to church!

The vociferous chick grew quickly and was soon ready for some outdoor activity. The first time Ginny took him for a walk, she discovered that the world was not ready for Bozo. Cats were only one of many strikes against him; Bozo had the uncanny ability of revealing the spirit of persecution dwelling in the hearts of many two-legged enemies around the neighborhood as well. People were extremely prejudiced against the adult plumage that unmistakably revealed his ancestry.

"Why do you have that dumb bird?" asked a neighbor.

"Why don't you just hit him over the head?" insisted a church man.

"He doesn't *deserve* to live, you know that, don't you?" announced a trusted friend.

"Don't you know what starlings *do*?" urged a teacher.

"Starlings are *bad* birds!" said a clerk, wagging her finger accusingly in Ginny's face.

"Hey! That's a *starling*," frowned a lady whom Ginny had often admired for her gracious Christian spirit. "Throw him *really hard* on the cement and bash in his skull!"

Every negative comment fueled Ginny's protective nature, and in spite of her resolve not to get attached, she was a little surprised to find herself fiercely in love with Little Bozo. She shuddered for him at every new criticism. Recalling several conversations at school with her two-legged fledglings, she began to realize that they, too, had faced the same ugly spirit. There truly were enemies lurking behind every bush! How could she "train up her children in the way they should go," Bozo included?

First, Bozo must learn to fly. Ginny gave him "the run of the house" at regular intervals. Too soon, the day arrived when Ginny knew that it was time to release her friend into the wild, but she didn't feel safe releasing him in her neighborhood—he was too tame, there were folks who did not like him, and there were cats who liked him way too much.

As always, Ginny prayed about what to do. Due to her kind protection, Bozo was unable to distinguish a friend from an enemy. What chance would he have to survive anywhere in the same city that had destroyed her beloved little Kelli? She kept her ears open for viable options, but came up empty-handed.

*What should I do? Bozo has got to face the world. It's not his fault he's a starling. Guide me...*

Just about the time Ginny was at her wits end about how to accomplish the safe release of her little black angel, someone suggested a bird sanctuary located a few hours away. Ginny dialed the number, but almost hung up before someone answered, fearful that they wouldn't want Bozo when they learned of his ancestry.

"Bird Sanctuary!" A lively young voice invited, "How may I help you?"

Ginny took a deep breath and began her sales pitch. "I have the most adorable adolescent bird who has been under my care for several weeks, now. I was wondering if you take young birds there?"

"Yes, we do! What kind of bird is it, Ma'am?"

Detecting a possible ally, Ginny increased the volume and velocity of her sales-pitch. "Oh you'll just *love* him! He is *so* good natured! He smiles *all* the time! I've named him Bozo because of his yellow lips. He *really* likes..."

"That's nice, Ma'am," the voice interrupted, trying to be patient. "But what *kind* of a bird *is* he?"

Ginny hadn't yet finished her list. She decided to talk faster, without taking a breath between sentences. "A neighbor girl found him near our yard and rescued him from some hungry cats, and you should see him when it's feeding time, and I've taught him everything he knows I've even taught him how to fly, and he sleeps right through the night, and..."

"That's nice, Ma'am," the voice was sounding a bit agitated, "But we *need* to know what *kind* of bird he is."

"Well…," Ginny knew that she had stalled as long as she could. Taking a deep breath she sighed and stated as quietly as possible, "He's a…," it was like admitting to her best friend that she had a terminal illness. She whispered, "…he's…he's a…*starling*."

In the moment of silence that followed, Ginny peppered the sanctuary official with her final estimation of Bozo's value. "…but he *thinks* he's an eagle, because I've been *telling* him that he's got the *heart* of an eagle, and I really think that he could *soar* with…"

"Wait," interrupted the voice from the sanctuary, "He doesn't *have* to be an eagle, Ma'am! We'll take him just as he is. And we'll love him no matter what!"

## Release

Ginny smiled in spite of the ache in her heart as she released Bozo. As he surveyed his new neighborhood, Bozo first perched in a tree right beside Ginny. When a group of starlings called to him he quickly flew upward, much higher than Ginny had ever seen him fly before. He did not fly as high as she had bragged, but his new home was everything she could have hoped for.

Ginny wiped away a tear and smiled to herself as she sent up a collective prayer for all the wounded and abandoned fledglings she had ever known—all the Jordans and Kellis, and all the Bozos, too. She prayed that they would find a safe haven, discover their wings, and fulfill their destiny.

Isn't it a comfort to know that there are some Ginny's in this old world that still put their arms around our gawky undesirables so naturally? You know the ones I mean—the youngsters in our schools, church families, and homes that sometimes sprout such odd-looking feathers that most of us can only stare, or raise a questioning eyebrow to each other behind their back? What if we were to learn how to believe in their destiny enough to at least acknowledge their presence? We would smile, ask their name, hug them if they wanted a hug, and then direct a word of encouragement into ears that were quite probably pierced by criticism long before those numerous rings appeared in them. Don't they need to hear what Ginny would have us say to them?

"It's OK, honey! You don't have to fly with eagles! I love you no matter what you are!"

---

All names in this story are pseudonyms.

# Weariness

God set him in a garden fair
Where tulips bloomed each spring;
About him always everywhere
Was many a lovely thing.
With miracle and mystery
His every day was filled,
And yet he only seemed to see
The structures mortals build.

He knew the stars were overhead,
But seldom raised his eyes,
The paths of life he chose to tread,
A stranger to the skies.
From youth to manhood, then to age,
He plunged his spirit deep
In figures on the ledger page,
Correct accounts to keep.

He never learned the names of flowers,
Or birds, or friendly trees,
In all his busy wakeful hours
He never heard the breeze
Enticing him with bits of song
To let a day go by
To watch a brooklet race along
Or gaze upon the sky.

God set him in a garden fair
With countless splendors strewn,
But all he saw while walking there
Was stone some man had hewn,
And all he talked was loss and gain
And cold commercial strife—
Which makes it easy to explain
How tired he grew of life.

—*Edgar Guest*

# When Stubby Spoke

*Thou hast created all things,
and for thy pleasure they were and are created.*

—Revelation 4:11

*A*s a young child, I wanted a bird so badly that I was willing to do almost anything to get one—even lie to my father. When I heard that someone wanted to give away a beautiful green and yellow budgie, I could hardly contain myself! Then, when the bird refused to speak as I expected, my childish heart lost interest in him. He was just not listening. But, now that I think back on it, maybe I wasn't listening.

"Oh, please Mamma!" I begged for the umpteenth time. "You'll never be sorry! I'll buy the seed! I'll keep his cage clean."

I had just turned nine when I learned of a budgie that was available for free—cage, seed, grit, and all—to a good home. I saw Mamma motion to her friend, Helen, not to mention anything about the "free bird" while I was within earshot, but it was too late. As usual, I was tuned in to the adult conversations going on around me rather than the children nearer my age at this gathering of friends.

For the next three days, I reminded Mamma every few minutes about the improbability of such a stroke of fate ever happening again—that such a bird's availability would so perfectly match my desire. I couldn't help it.

I had wanted a bird for as long as I could remember—almost as passionately as I had wanted a horse, but a horse required a country home.

I was born loving animals. I never played with dolls, but gravitated toward things warm, things covered with fur and feathers. Being a sickly child, I spent much of my time indoors. Finally, one doctor voiced the possibility that I might have some allergies. Sure enough, when tested, I was found to be exceptionally allergic—especially to fur and feathers!

I tried to content myself with the growing collection of miniature porcelain dogs and horses that my parents bought for me on special occasions. Daddy built me what he called a "shadow box" in which to display them, and they brought me much joy. I carefully studied the breeds of dogs and horses after which they were modeled, and tried to draw them. I had a goldfish, too, but it just wasn't the same as having a pet who could reciprocate my feelings. With only glass and fins offering me companionship, I felt deprived.

## Bird Passion

I remember the exact day that my natural attraction to birds was fanned into a passion. When I turned seven, Daddy took me to Dean Peter's house. "Pete," as Daddy called him, raised budgies. (His wife, Arlene, raised Arabians, but horses were out of the question.) I stood transfixed in Pete's aviary, a large screened room more than twenty feet square, with a cement floor. On three sides the walls were lined with nesting cages. The budgies were flying free, living rainbows all chirping, "Take me! Take me!" I pulled anxiously on Daddy's jacket, so he asked Pete the price of a budgie.

"Tell you what, Linda," said Pete, kneeling beside me, "You get ten classmates to pay you ten dollars each for a budgie and you can have yours for free!" So I did.

Well, not quite. I found nine kids that *said* they would buy one, but the tenth one eluded me. I knew I might be able to earn some extra money around the house so I added the tenth name: Lynn Hart. When I submitted the list to my father—all names, no money—it didn't fly.

## When Stubby Spoke

"This tenth name sounds a lot like your own, Linda Harper," he said raising an accusing eyebrow, "You wouldn't by any chance be trying to deceive me?" In the discipline that followed my confession, I lost all hope of ever having a budgie. That is, until I heard about "the free parakeet." Mamma was rightly concerned; I was always wheezing and coughing even if my fever drifted down toward normal on good days. She shook her head.

"No, Linda, I just don't think it would be a good idea for you to have a bird. The doctor said to stay away from fur and feathers, remember?"

"I won't *hold* him, Mamma. I'll just *look* at him!" I reasoned desperately. "Besides, I can give him away if he makes me sick!"

Reluctantly, Mamma finally gave in. She obtained the phone number from Helen and inquired if the budgie was still available.

"Yes, we still have the budgie. We are moving out tomorrow. Can you come this evening?" When Daddy came home from work, the whole family piled into our old Henry J and drove to the bird's house. By the time we arrived, I was so excited that I was struggling to keep my breathing under control. I can still see the man handing Daddy the bird of my dreams. It looked like he gave us enough birdseed for a year. As we left, he told us that his name was Stubby.

I held the cage in my lap all the way home. At last! My very own bird—the most beautiful bird in the world! He was a brilliant green with a yellow head and little black dots on either side of his beak. His long black, iridescent tail was too long to be entirely contained in the cage. I vowed to qualify as "the good owner" that this unselfish family had so desired for their bird. I didn't know that this bird was destined to teach me a very special lesson, but it was one that I would not be able to absorb until much later.

## Devotion Goes Awry

We spent many enjoyable hours together, Stubby and me. After school, I would let Stubby out of his cage to fly around my bedroom for awhile. He'd chirp happily from the drapery rod above my bed while I changed into my outdoor clothes. Then I would clean his cage, and give him fresh seed and water. When it was time for him to return to his cage, I would take out the long dowel that Daddy had given me and hold it up in front of Stubby. He would jump onto it and I would put him back in his cage.

Sometimes I read to him and he would chirp happily back to me at what seemed proper intervals. I adored that little bird; even his droppings looked artistic! I was fiercely protective; my siblings could look at Stubby, but I was the boss. Nothing bad was going to happen to *my* bird.

## Speak to Me

We had a large collection of children's records, which my two little sisters played repetitively. One song in particular inspired me to re-write one of the songs, inserting Stubby's name.

### When Stubby Spoke

*There's a boy who lives next door to me,*
*He's happy as can be;*
*Got a parakeet for his birthday,*
*Now he sings merrily—*

*Little Stubby Parakeet*
*Play with me, stay with me,*
*Night and day with me.*
*Though you walk like a parrot,*
*And talk like a bird,*
*I understand every single word.*

*Little Stubby parakeet, I love thee,*
*Happy little friends we'll always be.*
*I love my cat and my puppy dog, too,*
*And, little Stubby parakeet, I love you.*

"…and talk like a bird…" I pondered that statement.

"Mamma, can parakeets talk?"

"Yes," she replied. "A few years ago I heard one repeat 'pretty bird' whenever his owner said it to him."

I decided Stubby would learn to talk, too. I spent hours telling him what a "pretty boy" he was. He seemed to already know this because he spent plenty of time jabbering joyfully in budgie-talk to his mirror image, but he would not say the words in English. My fervent "good bye" and "see you later" brought no response from him, either. I finally shortened my message to one word, saying "hello" to him at least a hundred times a day. He seemed to enjoy the attention, but after about two weeks of repetition, I lost hope of Stubby ever learning to speak.

I reasoned that if he refused to learn my language, I would not speak to him. Without that interaction, I spent less time with him each day. I kept Stubby fed and watered, but my incentive to make his life happy was gone. Memorable moments ceased to accumulate.

## Silent Stillness

One day, Stubby was not in his cage when I returned from school. I searched every room in our large three-story house, repeatedly calling his name. Finally, I plopped down on my bed, staring at his empty cage, a silent reminder of my failure. That's when I happened to notice that my goldfish was floating upside-down in his bowl.

Tearfully, I brought my fishbowl to Mamma who discarded the dead fish. As I replaced the clean bowl on my dresser, I noticed a long tail feather from Stubby on the floor. I ran the long, thin, iridescent feather across my cheek, then placed it in the fish bowl. It wasn't until I saw several smaller green feathers on the other side of the bed that the sickening premonition washed over me; Stubby hadn't escaped, and he wasn't hiding. He had met with foul play.

I went outside to where my three-year-old sister was playing in the sandbox. I removed my socks, and sat on the brick retaining wall beside her, the feel of the sand comforting me as I considered my distresses.

"Hi Ninna," said Cindy, her big blue eyes registering some trouble of the heart. Her beach pail was in her lap, and her little red plastic shovel clutched in a chubby hand.

"Hi Thinny," I said, using the lisped rendition of her name. "My fish died."

"Th-tubby played with him today."

"Stubby killed my fish?" My lungs burned. I jabbed some jagged designs in the sand with a stick as I considered the ugliness of fang and claw. That's when it occurred to me that Cindy's wild beige and white cat, Sugar, was not in the sandbox as usual.

"Where is Sugar?" I asked. Cindy's eyes clouded, her chin began to quiver. She put her thumb in her mouth and started twisting her left pigtail. This habit, apparently, supported her thinking process, so I knew she was formulating a relevant commentary. I waited until I thought her thumb adequately moist enough to articulate a thought, then gently removed it from her mouth. Her adorable little rosebud mouth opened.

## When Stubby Spoke

"He fa don 'n die," she mumbled.

I didn't explore the sinister details about how Sugar "fell down and died"; there was something more important to do. We cried quietly together, our tears making little wet depressions in the sand at our feet. Finally, I asked one last question.

"Was Sugar in the house today?" The thumb was re-installed, and the pigtail propelled. Yes, my little sister had witnessed the unfortunate collision of two worlds.

There are a few stories from my childhood that I cannot recall without regret; one of those is the saga of Stubby. Whenever I see a green and yellow budgie, I can't help but think of Stubby. I try to remember our happy times, but my judgmental attitude regarding his speaking disability and his untimely demise overshadow the joy.

One day, as I was caring for my beautiful canaries and their colorful offspring, and blowing the hulls from their seed dishes, I found myself humming a few lines from my own rendition of that old childhood song, "Little Stubby Parakeet, play with me, stay with me, night and day with me..." As the hulls flew, I wondered if I had even given Stubby enough to eat. Sometimes a seed dish that looks full carries no nutrition.

"Oh, Stubby, I was irresponsible. I neglected you. If it looked like you still had some seeds in your feeder, I didn't add any fresh seeds. Maybe you had only empty hulls on some days. Maybe you were hungry?" I couldn't detect an answer.

"Some days I didn't refresh your water either." Silence.

"I'm sorry, Stubby. Please forgive me for not being there for you. You depended on me. I was young and uncaring." I saw him clearly in my mind's eye; the way he used to cock his head, then sneeze and mutter.

My old rocking chair creaked softly as the memories burned their way through my thoughts. Tears threaded their way down my cheeks as I absently thumbed through the stack of index cards noting my breeding canary pairs and their offspring. It had been a good year; 123 chicks in the large flight cage so far. That was the instant Stubby spoke to me. The message was in bird talk, and I had only recently become a subscriber, but I got the memo.

"Should you be adding to a population of birds who are totally dependent upon human fallibility?" I listened, then. I really listened. After all those years, Stubby delivered a significant note.

I no longer raise birds. Our flight cage is much larger now; that's what my husband, Jere, calls the miscellaneous array of bird feeders that he has hung from the support beams of our south porch. He is very careful to keep his seed buffet filled to assist the wild birds through the winter months, making sure that someone tends them if we are away. I have seen him pack a heavy bag of sunflower seeds nearly a quarter of a mile through knee-deep snow to make sure that "his birds" don't go hungry.

Our birds now build their own nests, with no help from us (though I sometimes supply them with a bit of lint from the filter on the drier) and raise their own chicks without our assistance. Occasionally we rescue one now and then, and they pay us back in color and song, and by keeping the grasshoppers out of our garden!

The old "Bird Room" nurtures another kind of life, now; numerous tables and lights afford an inviting place to plant seeds in January and February, giving us a jump-start on our greenhouse season that begins in mid-March while snow is still piled high against the trusses. As I write this, there are well over a hundred trays of plants in the space that we now call the "Green Room": petunias, marigolds, lobelia, pansies, violas, salvia, snapdragons, tomatoes, and many other young plants including the vegetables with which we feed ourselves and others. Though snow covers the frozen ground outside where the temperatures often hover at twenty below, the seedlings stay warm indoors. By getting a head start, they will become colorful bedding plants for use in baskets, patio pots, and vegetables gardens here in Canada's Far North.

On the wall of my Green Room is a plaque commemorating the day Stubby finally got through to me. In this unique representation of freedom, a lone seagull soars beneath a canopy of blue. I, myself, with one of Stubby's elegant tail-feathers, might have composed the three simple lines that complete this plaque if I'd not been so selfish. I thought of Stubby as *mine*.

*When Stubby Spoke*

*If you love something very much, let it go free.*
*If it comes back to you, love it forever.*
*If it does not return, it was not meant to be.*

—Anon

You know what I've discovered? Plants share their secrets, too! I wasn't expecting to communicate with them, but I'm becoming multi-lingual—with the help of my heart and my inner ear.

---

Indoor birds do have their place. Research accumulated by Dr. Marty Becker in his book, *The Healing Power of Pets* (Subtitle: *Harnessing the Amazing Ability of Pets to Make and Keep People Happy and Healthy*), is an excellent source of confirmation of why and how we find comfort in our pets; sometimes even diagnoses of disease, helpful therapy, as well as that healing bond! Required reading!

# My Garden is a Pleasant Place

My garden is a pleasant place
Of sun glory and leaf grace.
There is an ancient cherry tree
Where yellow warblers sing to me,
And an old grape arbor where
A robin builds her nest, and there
Above the lima beans and peas
She croons her little melodies,
Her blue eggs hidden in the green
Fastness of that leafy screen.

Here are striped zinnias that bees
Fly far to visit; and sweet peas,
Like little butterflies newborn,
And over by the tassled corn
Are sunflowers and hollyhocks,
And pink and yellow four-o'clocks.
Here are hummingbirds that come
To seek the tall delphinium—
Songless bird and scentless flower
Communing in a golden hour.

There is no blue like the blue cup
The tall delphinium holds up,
Nor sky, nor distant hill, nor sea,
Sapphire, nor lapis lazuli.
My lilac trees are old and tall;
I cannot reach their blooms at all.
They send their perfume over trees

And roofs and streets, to find the bees.
I wish some power would touch my ear
With magic touch and make me hear
What all the blossoms say and so
I might know what the winged things know.

I'd hear the sunflower's mellow pipe,
"Goldfinch, goldfinch, my seeds are ripe!'
I'd hear the pale wisteria sing,
"Moon moth, moon moth, I'm blossoming!"
I'd hear the evening primrose cry,
"Oh, firefly, come, firefly!"
And I would learn the jeweled word
The ruby-throated hummingbird
Drops into cups of larkspur blue,
And I would sing them all for you!

My garden is a pleasant place
Of moon glory and wind grace.
O friend, wherever you may be,
Will you not come and visit me?
Over fields and streams and hills,
I'll pipe like yellow daffodils,
And every little wind that blows
Shall take my message as it goes.
A heart may travel very far
To come where its desires are,
Oh, may some power touch my ear,
And grant me grace, and make you hear!

*—Louise Driscoll*

# Roady, the Road Runner

*Surely he shall deliver thee from the snare of the fowler,
and from the noisome pestilence.*

—Psalm 91:3

*If only she could escape from her city home in California, my friend, June, was sure that she would find fulfillment in gardening. When she was finally able to move to a country home, it was not only her garden in the small desert oasis that helped her find what she needed, but an injured bird who came to her for help. It's an unlikely story, but it happened, just like she told me.*

My young lemon tree looked like I felt; wilted. I was dragging the hose over to give it a drink when I first saw the road runner. He was much less shy than the others I had seen out in this Arizona desert country where I was trying to create a sanctuary; a garden oasis from my too-busy way of doing things back in California.

It seemed to be working. In my garden I was discovering that patience was one of the secrets of healthy growth, something that I knew I needed. There was a new object lesson every day as I planted, trained, pruned, and harvested my efforts.

Back in the city, I had rushed around like a road runner myself, attempting numerous tasks every day, but in a constant state of unrest. I did accomplish jobs, but not in a tolerant frame of mind. Here, out in the country, my soul and body were beginning to heal, but I was impatient for my heart garden to mature. Too often, when a problem challenged me, I found myself longing for the familiar services available in the city. Out in the country it seemed it took longer to live each day; sometimes I had to solve three or four problems just to water my garden. I couldn't efficiently just check things off of my list. In the city, there had been someone to do household repairs. Now I did them myself, sensing, in spite of my tendency toward impatience, that getting the job done was of less import than finishing my character. I needed to learn to relax, demand less, open my eyes to the bigger picture. That's where Roady came in.

Observing the road runners was becoming part of my healing. Watching the speedy birds as they darted through the mesquite, reminded me so much of the comic version that I just couldn't help smiling, and sometimes laughing aloud. When they ran after a lizard, they would flatten right out, long neck stretched forward, long tail straight out behind. Even their topknot would flatten when they ran!

The youngster behind my dehydrated lemon tree, however, did not run. He walked slowly away. I had a vague sense of concern for him, but by the time I had the hose properly positioned under the dry tree, he was gone.

I saw him again, the bird I decided to call Roady, a day or two later when I was trying to learn serenity. I needed a mouthwatering photo for the students attending the Master Gardener class I was teaching in Lake Havasu City. Determined that my garden become the Eden I had desired, I was digging a six-inch deep trench around the entire area in which to lay a chicken wire barrier to prevent the rabbits from feasting on my lettuce. Out of the corner of my eye, I saw Roady again, but this time he was beneath my lime tree, and near enough that I could see that his left foot was held at a strange angle. Ah, he was crippled; that was why he didn't run away like the others!

"You can live here with me, Roady!" I invited as I slowly approached him. He cocked his head sideways but remained where he was. "You can even live inside the garden fence if you want. The coyotes can't get you there! You can eat the snakes and lizards and all the other critters that take me by surprise when I'm working out here. I'll give you water. I'll feed you, whatever you need. Poor baby, your foot is hurt! I'll take care of you." He listened to my invitation, but stayed beyond my reach. I left him there in the shade of the lime tree, staring after me.

After eating lunch, I returned to my garden with a bundle of wire with which to secure my new barricade. I was ecstatic to see that Roady was still there! As I approached, he limped away very slowly, stopping in the shade of my lavender bush. I noticed, as I worked, that as long as I was on my knees, he was comfortable with me being less than ten feet from him, but when I stood up, he would raise his tail straight up and make a loud clacking noise with his beak. It sounded like a small firecracker or two pieces of wood quickly hitting together five or six times. If I knelt down and backed away, he would slowly lower his tail. Eventually he sought the shade of a creosote bush and peeked out from behind my iris.

I decided to see how close I could get if I stayed low. He refrained from clacking his beak until I was right beside the iris, a mere five feet from him. Then, he stopped clacking and stared quietly at me. I remained still. He clacked his beak again. Then, to my utter amazement, he took several steps toward me! When I slowly extended my hand, he backed away a little, but he had come close enough that I was better able to discern his foot problem; he was tangled in some string from the shade cloth that I had spread over the garden. A portion of the material had been tattered by the wind and had blown out of the enclosure. I was responsible for crippling this bird! Everything else could wait. I called my next-door neighbors, Arnie and Karen, to see if they would like to become honorary members of Road Runner Rescue.

"I figure if I can catch him, you can cut the strings off," I explained. Arnie and Karen were at my place in no time, eager to help.

By now, Roady was under a trellis laying flat on his tummy. I walked slowly toward him. Arnie, scissors in hand, followed a few steps behind me. Roady remained where he was. I squatted down, talked softly to him, and remained perfectly still for a few seconds. Then Roady let me just pick him up! He didn't fight a bit. In fact, he relaxed in my hands. Miraculously, it seemed he had no fear.

I stroked him and spoke gently, in what I hoped were reassuring tones. His speckled brown feathers were rough and hard. His body seemed to shrink into my right hand while I encircled his neck with the thumb and index finger of my left hand.

Arnie began carefully snipping the tough, black threads and I realized that this would be a lengthy process. The threads were not just on Roady's foot, they wound around and around the poor creature's entire body. Arnie and I positioned our chairs facing each other, with Karen taking pictures.

The bird remained relaxed, all eight-inches of body and twelve-inches of tail, even when Arnie began cutting the threads that entangled Roady's feet. The string was embedded in his legs and toes. Arnie's face was within inches of Roady's long, curved beak while making sure each line was severed completely. Roady's black eyes, encircled with a bright yellow rim, stared at me, unblinking. When his top knot began to rise, I would speak soft, encouraging words and it would slowly relax again.

In spite of the fact that Karen had recently fallen and broken both of her wrists, she was not content to just take pictures. After a few minutes of watching our struggle, she said, "I think my seam ripper would make this an easier job!" Cradling her heavy plaster casts, she hurried off in search of the instrument. I doubted she would be able to pick it up when she found it, for only the tips of her fingers showed beyond the edge of her casts, but find it she did, and the seam ripper was, indeed, easier on all of us.

When Roady was finally free, I turned him on his tummy and continued stroking him. He just laid there in my lap. Arnie handed my camera to Karen who captured proof that I had actually petted a road runner! Then I laid the bird in his lap while Karen took more pictures. She couldn't resist touching Roady with the tips of her fingers. Still Roady lay quietly in Arnie's lap.

When we had our fill of loving Roady, I set him on the ground. When he realized his was no longer tangled, he became a different bird. He fluffed his feathers and quickly ran under the wheelbarrow. When I peeked underneath, he clacked his beak, flattened his topknot, lowered his tail, and bolted for the desert!

Once or twice a day I see him patrolling the garden fence. No more limping. I can't get quite as close to him, but he hangs around to thank me in his own way. After a good running start, he will glide over the garden fence and inspect my plants for lizards and other tasty morsels that find their way into my garden.

He seems to know just when to show up; he comes right when I'm in the midst of a problem, right when I need to stop and smile. So, I lower my topknot and take time to "set a spell" with my little friend. Like Roady, I'm being cut free, too—one strand of stress at a time.

## Far from the Maddening Crowd

It seems to me I'd like to go
Where bells don't ring, nor whistles blow,
Nor clocks don't strike, nor gongs sound,
And I'd have stillness all around.

Not real stillness, just the trees
Low whisp'ring, or the hum of bees,
Or brooks faint babbling over stones,
In strangely, softly tangled tones.

Or maybe a cricket or katydid,
Or the songs of birds in the hedges hid.
Or just some such sweet sound as these,
To fill a tired heart with ease.

If 'twern't for sight and sound and smell,
I'd like the city pretty well,
But when it comes to getting rest,
I like the country lots the best.

Sometimes it seems to me I must
Just quit the city's din and dust,
And get out where the sky is blue,
And say, now, how does it seem to you?

—*Nixon Waterman*

# My Eagle

*"...I bare you on eagles' wings, and brought you unto myself."*

—Exodus 19:4

*I* met Patsy when we divided into small groups at a seminar. As we were learning about each other, I shared with her my love for uplifting bird stories, and she told me an amazing incident of how the world's most majestic bird encouraged her at the very lowest depth of her emotional suffering. It came at a time when she felt so alone that she was sure no one understood her plight and that even God couldn't fix her aching heart. This is the story of how my friend came to realize how special she was and how much her Father longed for her to soar to heights she'd never have known, but for the lessons learned in sorrow.

The children and I began our home-school days with the pledge of allegiance out beside the swimming pool. Together, we lifted our eyes upward to our beautiful red, white and blue flag and chorused, "...with liberty and justice for all." My eyes wandered beyond the flag to where, once more, "my eagle" was soaring. He was so far away that I could really only *hope* it was an eagle, for I could detect no identifying marks at that distance. To see "my eagle" while my family and I said our morning pledge—wings outstretched, soaring upward—always lifted my spirit to face the challenges of the day. My kinship with this iconic symbol of freedom was a long-standing affair. Why did I love eagles so much?

## My Eagle

### *Close-up and Free*

As a child, eagles were my favorite bird, but in my entire life I had seen only one live eagle close enough to distinguish any identifying marks. It was in a cage. I had never seen one in the wild, and to see a live eagle was one of my dreams. The chances of observing an eagle close-up and free near where we lived, out in the dry panhandle of Oklahoma with no significant body of water within a fifty-mile radius of our desert home, was impossible, of course. I might as well hope to find a gold nugget in our back yard! In spite of the improbability, however, the longing in my heart persisted; would "my eagle" someday reveal himself to me?

For three years I'd been unable to climb out of my tailspin. Family complications had taken their toll. My joy was gone. The distant eagle, as we said the pledge of allegiance together, had become a vital object lesson of hope—"my eagle" was soaring above entanglements. That's what I wanted. I'd read books about healing journeys. Joy *seemed* reachable, but somehow I just could not rise above the discouragement that had convinced me that I was of little worth to anyone, even to God.

Then, one day in a bookstore, I stumbled across a book about eagles. I was riveted. Among other facts, it explained how eagles are attracted to water. I so desired to have an eagle visit me that I actually considered stocking our swimming pool with trout! But our pool is always the focal point of family gatherings, so I gave up on that idea. I cherished our family time together. There were eight of us that gathered around our large dining table three times a day. Even my husband came home for meals. We went to church together twice a week, too. I taught children's classes at church. I stayed busy. I smiled at everyone. As a family, we appeared to have it all, but no one knew about the hole in my heart through which I felt my life slowly draining. I didn't really understand why I could not break free. I felt as if I was being smothered or choked, and that I would die of sorrow. I finally tried talking to my husband about it.

"Some days I feel as if I will die from sadness," I complained to him. "There are so many things that are right, but this one thing is so wrong, so big, that it swallows up every good thing. How can I know God's love while I'm being crushed by the weight of this burden?"

"I wish I could help, Patsy," he tried to console me, "but I think this is something you and the Lord will have to sort out."

I was left feeling totally deflated, as if no one understood or cared about my sorrow.

## Does He Care?

The very next week, our pastor delivered a heartfelt message to the congregation about how we need to examine certain characteristics of salvation, one of which is the aspect of bearing fruit. How could I determine what kind of fruit I was bearing? Mine was not the right kind of fruit—maybe sour grapes? The question troubled me. I felt like such a hypocrite. I knew that God was real, but I just couldn't feel the assurance of His love for me. Like Jacob, I found myself grappling with God in a desperate struggle for peace.

*Am I really saved, Lord? Do I really belong to you? Sweeten the fruit I am bearing! Let me know You love me! Please?*

I was repeating this silent, desperate plea on our way home from church one afternoon, trying to recall the words of some encouraging hymns: *Does Jesus care when your heart is sad? Heartaches, take them all to Jesus,* and *Happiness is the Lord.* But no matter how I tried to shore up my faith, I still ached, head to toe, with a desperate longing for approval and love. I was as low in spirit as I have ever been. Fortunately, that was about to change.

## On Eagles' Wings

From my position in the front seat beside my husband, I could see the vast expanse of clear blue Oklahoma sky stretching out above us, brilliant and serene. We had a forty-mile ride ahead of us, and there would

## My Eagle

be little traffic. I was tempted to close my eyes in hopes of silencing my despair. I'm so thankful I did not give in to that impression; if I had been sleeping I would have missed the life-altering experience that the Lord had planned!

About midway into our journey homeward, I detected a shadow overtaking our vehicle from behind. Soon, the huge form of an eagle, his wings fully as wide as the car and held motionless in a powerful glide, slowly passed above us at a height of less than ten feet! He soared just ahead of us as if escorting us. Was I seeing things? No! There was his great white head, and then came the distinctive white tail.

"My eagle!" I blurted. "Oh, look! It's my eagle!" For about a quarter of a mile the eagle stayed with us, then he slowly began climbing upward. I barked a command through the constriction in my throat.

"Stop the car! Stop the car!" I jumped out and watched my eagle for as long as I could. Staring upward, hands across my chest in an unconscious effort to retain this celestial moment, I was oblivious to the tears streaming down my face.

Then he was gone. Well, not really gone; I just couldn't see him anymore, but his message stayed with me.

*You are under the shadow of My wings, my precious daughter. If you let me, I will bear you up on eagles' wings. You are never alone. Do not give in to the temptation to doubt my love for you. Whatever you bear, I bear it with you. Give me your burden.*

My heart was so full of joy that I could barely breathe! My husband understood a significant portion of what this encounter meant to me. The rest of my family seemed a little embarrassed at my outburst, but were happy for "Mom's meaningful moment."

## Daily Reminder

Not long ago my husband replaced our sagging flagpole. Imagine my delight to find, perched magnificently atop our new pole, a golden replica of my eagle! I am reminded, every day during our pledge of allegiance, about my encounter.

Oh, at times I get discouraged, but I no longer fall into utter despair. Whenever I see a speck soaring in the distant sky, I am reminded of "my eagle." Conviction warms me, from the top of my head to the soles of my feet. What a messenger! What a message!

# From the Hand of Love

It is He who made the flowers and
who gave to the sparrow its song who says,
"Consider the lilies," "Behold the birds."
In the loveliness of the things of nature you may learn more
of the wisdom of God than the schoolmen know.
On the lily's petals, God has written a message for you,
written in language that your heart can read
only as it unlearns the lessons of distrust
and selfishness and corroding care.

Why has He given you the singing birds and the gentle blossoms,
but from the overflowing love of a Father's heart,
that would brighten and gladden your path of life? …
He has filled the earth and air and sky with glimpses of beauty
to tell you of His loving thought for you.
The beauty of all created things is but a
gleam from the shining of His glory.

—*Ellen White*

# Love Tap

*"...those that seek me early shall find me."*

—Proverbs 8:17

When our son, Jed, married petite, graceful, athletic Amber, who also sang like a nightingale, I discovered an ever-increasing level of joy. When Amber mentioned to me that they'd had a special little guest visiting them on a regular basis, I was more than curious to hear the details. Her revelation was as thrilling as any I have recorded. I'll begin where her story commenced to take shape under a dark cloud several weeks before....

Amber's marriage had been ordained of God, she'd never doubted that. The first time she saw Jed, she found her heart responding to his easy-going ways, his ability to solve problems, and his mature spiritual commitment. She allowed herself to think about him, but in a controlled manner.

*If it's in God's plan, I could love that young man.*

There had been tests along the way, but the trials only served to remove any doubt she might raise with regard to Jed's sterling integrity. Now, Amber was living the dream she'd desired from early childhood—a loving husband who believed strongly in God and country living; two darling children who enthusiastically helped with farm and home chores, and who adored sitting on her lap for story time asking wide-eyed questions about their expected sibling. Life was perfect.

What, then, was this strange and unwelcome cloud that was overshadowing her usual happiness? Was it just a species of "cabin fever" after those three days of rain that had kept them all cooped up in their motorhome at S. R. Farms*? No, it was deeper than that. The darkness had been gathering for several weeks, and it was not like Amber to be the least bit gloomy.

## Identifying the Impasse

Some folks might tend to think that Amber was overworked, but there's nothing more enjoyable to her than climbing into bed at night with a sense of accomplishment after a busy day on the farm. While her third pregnancy had made the usual demands on her system, things that she had always been able to accomplish easily had become nearly overwhelming. Something was draining her energy, something other than a physical malady.

After a few days of deep soul-searching, Amber decided that the shadow had gathered almost imperceptibly as the ever-increasing demands of her growing family edged in on her morning devotional and exercise time. God was tenderly calling her back to spend that cherished sacred hour of spiritual and physical training that was so necessary to her peak performance. Although some mornings she was able to read a little, it was not as much as she needed because she could not seem to focus—mentally or physically. She felt alone in the struggle to energize her spiritual life. Her only available "quiet time" was while the rest of the household was asleep in the morning. When Jed expressed his concern, she was desperate enough that she finally confided her dilemma to him.

"Jed, why can't I read when I first wake up, like you do?" Amber asked. "It would be so much easier to schedule my personal devotions if only my eyes would focus quickly, but the words are so blurry! I can't read in bed like you do. I have to wash my face, comb my hair, dress, and get my circulation started. If I close my eyes, thinking that I will rest them while I pray, I almost always fall back to sleep and miss my golden opportunity."

"I thought everyone could read when they first woke up." Jed hugged her. "Sorry your eyes don't focus, Amber. But, you'll figure this out. I know you will!"

That evening, after tucking the children into bed, she again set her alarm hoping to rise early enough for a brisk walk in the invigorating morning air and then read awhile before she fixed breakfast. When her alarm rang, she was tempted to stay snuggled in the warm comfort of Jed's strong arms, but she willed her left foot to examine the coolness outside of the blankets. The right foot followed, and slowly, her body rose to greet the day. As she dressed, she prayed.

*I want to see with Your eyes, Lord. If I could see as You see, I could surely focus. Please bless my exercise time. Keep my thoughts on You, for I long to know You better.*

Walking briskly down the freshly graveled driveway where their grain bins were still brimming with their high-grade, over-wintered organic oats, her heart surged with gratefulness that Jed's new farming venture was going so well. Her song joined that of the birds as she turned homeward. By the time she returned, her eyes were as fully open as her heart.

Following the new schedule, Amber's clouds began to lift. When she missed a day, they returned. The night Jed and Amber returned home to Sanctuary Ranch (located two hours from their grain farm), she again set her alarm for 5 a.m. and prayed earnestly to maintain her program of exercise and reading.

*Lord, I so enjoy exercising early, taking time with Your Word, but I still struggle getting up early. I wish it was easier for me to awaken, but thank You for blessing me with the strength to keep my new schedule so far....*

## The Awakener

"Tap-tap-tap," came the dainty but insistent sound at their bedroom window that first morning back home. Amber looked toward the window. It was light, but her clock said she had nearly twenty minutes, yet, so she decided to rest until her alarm rang.

"Tap-tap-tap-tap-tap," the sound came again before she was fully asleep. Curious, Amber arose from her warm nest and shuffled across the chilly floor to the window hoping she might see an animal to show Jed. One of their favorite pastimes was observing wildlife that wandered through their yard, and morning was definitely the best time to watch the moose, deer, elk, coyotes, and bears. This, however, was not one of the bigger animals. A tiny yellow bird, his feathers fluffed in the cool morning air, was peeking in the bedroom window as if he was looking for someone. As Amber watched from the shadows, he tapped again.

*How sweet! I won't waken Jed for it will surely fly away. Hmmm…it's still only 4:45 a.m., but I'm awake. Might as well get dressed, go for a walk and have my devotional time a little early.*

The bird remained on the windowsill, singing and tapping as Amber dressed. She smiled at the feathered messenger, thinking some rather large thoughts as she muted her alarm clock so Jed could sleep a little longer. He had been putting in some long hours in the fields, and this was his chance to catch up on some much-needed rest.

*Interesting coincidence, that bird coming just before my alarm clock rang. It's more fun to rise to that tiny tapping sound than to the jarring buzz of my alarm clock.*

When the same little yellow bird tapped on the bedroom window the next morning, Amber began to wonder if this was more than a coincidence. When the bird awakened her again before 5 a.m. on the third morning, her heart was warming to new truth.

*Do birds actually listen to God in order to help people? My mother-in-law believes strongly that God uses birds that way. I'll have to tell her about this when I see her today.*

At breakfast, she mentioned the bird to Jed, and was a little surprised that his smile reflected no trace of amusement when she expressed her theory.

"Amber, I've been having the same experience, only I asked the Lord to awaken me just before 6 a.m., because I don't feel a need of any more exercise than I get here. I didn't hear him tapping for you, but for the last three mornings, that same bird has been waking me up! I just *have* to get up and smile at him, and when I do, I am awake enough to do my reading...*in bed*," he grinned.

What he didn't tell Amber at that time was how very concerned he'd been for her. She was carrying a heavy load with two toddlers at her side and the new child forming within her. Even without her faithful housekeeping and cooking those delicious vegetarian meals he loved, her plate was full. He had found himself pleading for personal guidance on her behalf.

*"Lord, I know that I am doing the work You asked me to do in growing healthy food on the land You have provided. And I know it is the work Amber enjoys, but is it too much for her during these summer months? Do You want me to cut back? What should I do? If this is what we need to keep doing, then I need a sign from You."*

That prayer had again been in his heart the night they returned to the home ranch, just four days earlier. His father and I had taught Jed early to love country living and to keep his inner eye open to all of the lessons that the plants and animals would teach him. That first morning, when the little bird awakened him, a buried memory struggled to surface while he was reading his Bible.

*There's something familiar about that little bird. I don't know what kind it is...but I have seen it before...*

## Singing Messenger

The next morning, when the bird again tapped and sang to Jed, the memory came flooding back to him. This was the same kind of little yellow angel that had played a significant role in his decision to marry Amber! Being a burn survivor, Jed had wondered whether it was in God's plan for him to marry and have a family. His scars, the result of a gasoline explosion that nearly took his life at age eight, are significant.[†] During his healing years, Jed was the model of optimism, but during his later teens, he expressed his concern to me.

"Mom, who will love me now?" he'd ask me. "I'm all scarred up." I assured him that I had been praying about His soul mate for many years, even before his burn accident, and I was certain that God was in the business of happy marriages, and if Jed was willing to do it according to the model in Genesis 24, I was sure someone was being prepared for him. This someone would love the work Jed was called to do, and his scars would merely assist in the sifting process. At first, Jed resisted subscribing to the courtship method, fearing that the Lord may choose someone for him that he could not love.

Then, a family joined us in ministry. During the third year of their sojourn from Montana, Jed was convinced that their oldest daughter, Amber, was the one God had chosen for him. Jed asked his Dad, Jere, to approach Amber's father, Ron, with his request for a courtship. When, after several months, her parents had still not given their approval, Jed became seriously discouraged, questioning whether he should abandon hope. He was losing sleep, weight, and hair.

One Sabbath afternoon, in great heaviness of spirit, Jed decided to take some time alone. He hiked across the river that borders our acreage, ending up at the foot of a waterfall where he surrendered the burden of his heart, repeating his privately selected "courtship verse," Psalm 37:4: *Delight thyself also in the LORD; and he shall give thee the desires of thine heart.*

*Lord, it seemed obvious that it was Your will for me to inquire about a courtship with Amber, but that was so long ago I am tempted to think that I am not the one for her. I need some assurance. Please send me a sign of Your approval. I continue to wait on You in this regard....*

As Jed looked upward, a flash of yellow caught his attention. Like a sunbeam, it materialized through the leaves of a nearby cottonwood and illumined the ground at his feet. It was a tiny bird, not even as big as a canary. The bird hopped toward him as if it had been hand-raised. Totally unafraid, the bit of golden fluff looked up at Jed, cocked his head, then chirped and sang—directly to him!

Jed had helped me with several wild rescues as well as raising canaries and was used to handling birds, but this one was so tame that he half expected the warbler to jump up onto his shoulder! That day, the little bird "spoke" to him just as surely as if it had been written in the blue sky above the waterfall.

> *God sees my friend the sparrow, sweet,*
> *He guides this warbler, too.*
> *He knows your heart,*
> *He sees your tears,*
> *I know He cares for you!*
>
> *He cares for you!*
> *God cares for you!*
> *He heard your prayer today!*
> *This is my song,*
> *It won't be long,*
> *For He has heard you pray!*

## The Awakening

There, beside the pool at the foot of the falls, Jed carried on a very enlightening conversation with the warbler. He has no idea how long they communicated, for time stood still. All he knows is that when the bird flew up into a towering cottonwood nearby, the burden on his heart lifted, too. This was the sign his faith needed.

Less than a week later, he received approval from Ron to begin a courtship. He considered the visitor at the waterfall to have played a significant role in the unfolding of his own love story, encouraging him to quietly persevere, not lose hope in the outworking of His "deep designs."

Jed had kept his little golden angel very personal until the tapping occurred again on the third morning. When the memory returned in full, he shared with Amber what had happened at the foot of the waterfall prior to their courtship. They had cried together before, but this was the only tearful prayer of thankfulness in their seven years of marriage that had included a bird!

Sometime during the second week of morning visits from their little yellow angel, Jed and Amber woke Hannah and Andrew to share the excitement with them. Turning the pages of their bird guide, they discovered that their friendly little benefactor was, indeed, a yellow warbler. This little warbler, with the rusty stripes on his breast, is common in British Columbia, but generally very shy, and their song clearly identifies them, "Sweet-sweet-sweet-he's-so-sweet."

With the exception of two rainy mornings, this little bird tapped on their bedroom window for well over three weeks at the precise times that Jed and Amber had prayed to awaken for their devotional time! Isn't that, according to recent scientific research, about the amount of time it takes to form a habit? Their "awakening" became so commonplace that the weekend they went camping Amber half-expected to hear the bird tap on their tent flap Sabbath morning!

## Watching With New Eyes

Amber was excited the day she told me the story as we worked in the garden together. "It's easy to expect miracles, now," she said. "I listen and watch, with new eyes and ears, for little signs that I may be missing!"

Amber's lesson, even deeper than rising early enough to "exercise and focus," was the assurance that God was tenderly watching over her, turning her weakness into strength, her clouds into sunshine. He *is* there. He *does* care. If the heart is seeking truth, the eyes can be made to see what is otherwise unperceived.

*"For the invisible things of him from the creation of the world are clearly seen, being understood by the things that are made, [even] his eternal power and Godhead; so that they are without excuse"* (Romans 1:20).

Nothing is coincidence. God is in control. Jed and Amber are convinced!

---

\* www.onedegreeorganics.com: To learn about Jed and Amber's Peace Country grain farm.

† For the complete version of Jed's healing journey and touching love story, read *Rainbow in the Flames*.

# Did You Ever Hear an English Sparrow Sing?

What? an English sparrow sing?
Insignificant brown thing,
So common and so bold, 'twould surely bring
Tears of laughter to the eyes
Of the superficial wise
To suggest that that small immigrant could sing.

'Twas the bleakest wintry day,
Earth, sky, water, all were gray,
Of the universe old Boreas seemed king,
As he swept across the lake
But his empire was at stake,
When that little English sparrow dared to sing.

Not a friend on earth had I,
No horizon to my sky,
No faith that there could be another spring.
Cold the world as that gray wall
Of the Auditorium tall
Where I heard that little English sparrow sing.

On the shelving of one stone
He was cuddling all alone;
Oh, the little feet knew bravely how to cling!
As from out the tuneful throat
Came the sweetest, springlike note,
And I truly heard an English sparrow sing.

You may talk for all your days
In the thrush and bluebirds' praise
And all your other harbingers of spring,
But I've never heard a song
Whose echoes I'd prolong
Like that I heard that English sparrow sing.

Oh, my heart's a phonograph
That will register each laugh
And all the happy sounds that from the joy-bells ring,
So if cloudy days should come,
In my hours of darkest gloom
I'm sure I'll hear that English sparrow sing.

*—Bertha Johnston*

# Halo

*You have not chosen me, but I have chosen you....*

—John 15:16

When Walt told me about his young Amazon's special assignment, he had tears in his eyes. Although he and his family have raised hundreds of birds, they value each one as an individual with unique talents, convinced that each chick hatched in their aviary has a destiny to fulfill. Adoption is always a difficult time for them; matching a bird to the right owner is serious business, with none more challenging than the day Angelina rang their doorbell.

She wasn't that old, but Angelina looked ancient, fragile, exhausted. She had developed severe disabilities and was aging rapidly. The doctors could identify and temporarily relieve some of her symptoms, but could neither diagnose nor speculate in regard to her life span. Most troublesome was the rare type of arthritis that had left her with unrelenting pain. Although she received help with her daily needs, Angelina desired something more. It seemed to her that she had always needed something more, even before the physical pain began…some kind of reliable warmth and understanding by the friends and family that had deserted her; a connectedness that didn't fizzle out with time like the pain meds that stood at attention like well-ordered soldiers across her dresser.

One day, as she lay in bed in agony of heart, mind, and body, there came to her a picture. In her imagination she saw a bird, a brilliant green bird with understanding eyes, a hooked beak, and a hint of yellow on his head. Did such a creature exist? When she discovered that a family who raised parrots lived not far from her, she phoned for an appointment.

Walt and his wife, Doris, had begun raising parrots while their children were still in grade school. The birds and children developed a strong symbiosis. The aviary became a favorite field trip for church groups and grade school children. The birds were an endless source of object lessons for better living. The life expectancy of unstressed parrots exceeds 100 years. Children and adults alike noticed the wide variety of fresh foods on which the parrots thrived. Some were inspired to consider a fresher diet for themselves.

Parrots are devoted. Most parrots are dedicated caretakers of their young. They will often feed and protect their mate in the case of illness, and grieve over its death.

The parrot world reinforces the biblical account of creation by design through the beauty of feather, form and character...could this vibrant color combination just "happen"?

Walt and Doris discovered that their birds could differentiate several cars by the sound of the motor in the driveway, and would respond accordingly. If they liked the one who usually came to visit in that car, they would be happy; if not, they would hunker down in a corner of their cage. The birds learned to mimic laughter and knew when to use the sound appropriately. The older pairs used words to communicate their wants and could imitate the voices of family members—a cause for many humorous episodes in the aviary.

One of the toughest times in the household was when the young parrots were mature enough to be adopted out. The strengths and weaknesses of each bird were carefully studied for personality, adaptability, aggressiveness, and peculiar habit traits. Raising birds was not just a hobby for this family, it was a mission. They would never consider selling a bird to a family who was not prepared to make a lifetime commitment.

Then they met Angelina.

It was obvious that Angelina was failing. She was living one day at a time, if you could call it living. "Decrepit" was the word that came to Walt's mind the first time he saw the woman slouched low in her wheelchair on his front porch. Where some folks wear a smile, Angelina wore a grimace that expressed both pain and determination. Wheeling slowly from the porch into the living room, she shared her longing for companionship. Some type of emotional turmoil caused a level of cynicism, and bitter commentary laced its way into her conversation. Walt and Doris looked at each other; would any of their birds be able to fulfill this assignment? It would have to be a bird with a special empathy and dedication—almost a sense of mission, for Angelina was not your average client. Would their currently adoptable youngsters even notice her? Would Angelina be able to provide the care that a young bird needed?

"Angelina," Walt instructed, "I'm not sure how the birds will react to your wheelchair. We have seen them treat a person in a wheelchair as an inanimate object. Currently we have a clutch of three yellow-nape Amazons that we haven't shown to anyone yet. Doris will go get the birds and place them on the floor here in the living room. You wait patiently, without moving, and see if they notice you. If one happens to come toward you, slowly lower your hand to the floor in front of the bird. If he is so inclined, he may climb onto your hand. Just leave him there awhile until he becomes more familiar with you. Bonding takes time."

When Doris released the three young parrots about five feet in front of her wheelchair, Angelina pulled herself into a forward lean with obvious anticipation. Two of the birds, overwhelmed with their new world, huddled together shaking with fright. The third youngster looked around, immediately made eye contact with Angelina, and quickly hopped across the carpet toward her.

*Climbing the Heights*

Recognizing the bird of her dreams, Angelina extended the hand of friendship. When the bird jumped onto her hand Angelina instantly scooped him up next to her face, an aggressive action not recommended with a bird whose beak can break a finger!

Walt and Doris held their breath. This adoption was definitely not progressing in the usual manner. Angelina's nose was now within easy "striking range"! What would happen next?

The young parrot muttered a friendly greeting, hopped onto Angelina's shoulder and began gently preening the short hairs along the back of her neck—an advanced form of affection. Walt and Doris breathed a collective sigh of relief and soon returned the young birds to their nest. The meeting was much too short for both Angelina and the young green parrot with the touch of yellow on his head.

"Come back at this time next week and we'll see what happens," said Walt, not convinced that the bonding they had just witnessed could be permanent.

Hope lit a fire in Angelina's heart, and the blaze increased through the week, replacing a portion of her pain with a warm sense of anticipation. She was plenty early for her appointment the next week, trembling with excitement, an expectant sparkle lighting her eyes. Doris brought the same clutch of young Amazons and released them a little farther from the wheelchair this time. The same two cowered together, but the third parrot immediately hopped over to Angelina and did his best to communicate in baby parrot talk: "Oh *there* you are! I thought I'd *lost* you! Where'd you *go*, anyway?"

Angelina closed her eyes in ecstasy when, just as before, the parrot climbed onto her hand, quickly sidestepped to her shoulder, and played with her hair. This time, though, he moved to her face, preened her eyebrows, and began a close inspection of her glasses.

Angelina made payment in full and took her bird home that day. Reports from Angelina were always upbeat, so when they did not hear from her, they assumed things were progressing favorably. Walt was caught off-guard several months later, when Angelina phoned with distressing news.

"I need to allow Halo a chance at a second home," Angelina said huskily.

"Oh, Angelina!" Walt exclaimed. "Is Halo giving you trouble, now?"

"No, no! That's not it at all!" Angelina's voice softened with the hint of a sob. "Halo was born to love...he was born to love *me*! He's just what I needed. He's been such a comfort! I can't begin to thank you enough for entrusting him to me."

"But...you want to bring him back?"

"It's time...," Angelina choked out after a long pause. "Time for me to let go. I'm...dying, Walt. I can't care for my dear little pal properly, now."

Angelina had learned life-changing lessons from Halo by his continual expressions of unconditional love. He had so softly, steadily, and proficiently pecked away at the blinders of self-centeredness that, even as her body was fading, Angelina had morphed into a new person. Walt sensed it in her voice. Halo's God-given love had so sweetened her bitter cup that even the dregs had become palatable.

"Oh, Angelina! I'm so very sorry to hear that. He can come back whenever it is convenient for someone to bring him."

How was little Halo capable of understanding his destiny? His assignment seemed crystal clear to him from the very first day he met his wheelchair lady. He knew what she needed, and he set about convincing his lady that she was loved. The hardest job he had was to persuade his family before it was too late for him to accomplish his calling!

Though it had been a struggle for Halo's caring family to release him into Angelina's care, Walt and Doris are sure they made the right decision. And, though they are at a loss to explain this remarkable case of affinity, they cannot deny that their little angel earned his beautiful golden crown. If only for a few short months, Halo brought purpose into the life of a young woman who had become sullen and resentful. He was a true friend; and only a true friend could so effectively dull the jagged edge of grief with the joy of realizing that life was worthwhile before she was called to her rest. Perhaps Halo was the only one from whom she could have learned that most valuable lesson.

*Only the soul that knows the mighty grief
can know the mighty rapture.*

—Edwin Markham

---

All names in this story are pseudonyms.

# Love on the Wild Side

*by Penny Porter*

*The richness of the human experience would lose something of rewarding joy if there were no limitations to overcome.*

—Helen Keller

It was one of those unforgettable mornings, jouncing along twisting cattle trails and dirt roads on our Arizona Hereford ranch, that we came across the mourning doves. Pegged out like clothespins along miles of sagging telephone wires, their sunlit feathers reflected rainbows in the early glow of dawn, but, bead-bright eyes were riveted on our pickup load of grain.

"Dumbest birds on earth!" Bill grumbled as he pulled up beside the first of six 18-foot aluminum feed troughs.

"Why do you always call them dumb, Daddy?" Jaymee asked.

"Because doves are out to kill themselves before they even hatch." He struggled to light his pipe, a familiar sign that he had more to say. "They fly into window panes and break their necks. They lean over too far and drown in stock tanks." He climbed from the truck and hauled an 80-pound sack of grain onto his shoulder. "And they build nests with such big holes in the bottom, they wouldn't hold a Ping-Pong™ ball, let alone an egg."

Then how come so many survive? I wondered as I watched him buck his way through the herd of milling cattle, rip open the sack and begin to pour.

Alerted by the clatter of grain, doves suddenly darkened the sky. We heard the surge of whistling wings, and the phantom-rush of air as they swooped down in a frenzied quest for corn. Some lit on the cows' horns. Others blanketed their backs. But most silvered the earth like a restless sea around the stomping cattle hooves.

Suddenly, Jaymee screamed, "Daddy! That cow's standing on a dove's wing!"

Bill tossed an empty feed sack into the back of the pickup and hurried toward the cow. "Dumb bird," he muttered as he twisted the cow's tail till she shifted her weight. The dove was free, but one wing lay on the ground, severed from its body at the shoulder.

I don't know how long we watched the pathetic creature flapping its remaining wing and spin in useless circles as though winding itself into the ground. At last it tipped forward, beak in the dirt, and mercifully lay still.

Thank God! I thought, torn between scrambled emotions of sadness and relief. It's dead. After all, there was nothing we could do for a bird with only one wing.

Bill nudged the dove with the toe of his boot. Horrified, we watched it flip onto its back wild-eyed with pain. Jaymee's small hands flew to her lips. "Oh, no!" she cried. "It's still alive! Daddy, do something!"

Bill leaned down and wrapped the tiny, broken creature in his red handkerchief, and handed it to Jaymee. "Here, honey," he said, "you'll have to hold it till we get home."

"But it's going to die!" I heard the tremor of fear in her voice.

"I don't think so," he said. "They're even..." I caught his eye and defied him to say, "...too dumb to die."

"What are we going to do with it, Mama?" Jaymee's brow was creased with worry. Only eight years old, she loved small animals and was forever rescuing soft, fluffy kittens; baby rabbits; and ground squirrels. But this was different. This was a bird. Furthermore, it was grotesquely wounded.

"We'll put it in a box, give it water and grain." I stopped right there, knowing too well that the rest was up to God.

Sorrow clouded her small face. "But if it lives, it won't ever be able to fly again, and it'll have to live in a cage—forever."

"Lots of birds do," I said.

"But that's canaries and parakeets...and they're pretty...." Then in a whisper she added, "...and they're *smart*."

On our way back to the house Jaymee sat quietly between us holding the young dove in her lap. Deep in thoughts of her own, she stroked its tiny head with two fingers until she walked into the kitchen where Becky, her ten-year-old sister was eating breakfast. She showed her the bird. "A cow chopped its wing off," she told her.

Becky wrinkled her nose but later, after helping bed a shoe box with dried grass and placing the bird near the woodstove for warmth, she asked, "What are you going to name it?"

"Olive," Jaymee said.

"Olive! That's an awful name. Why Olive?"

"Because Noah's dove flew all the way back to the ark with an olive branch...and that wasn't so *dumb*."

While the girls were in school, I listened for sounds of life from the box, and repeatedly peeked inside at the tiny, gray, ghostlike creature hiding in the dark, head drooped, rainbows gone. I found a jar of antibiotic salve in the barn. "For Olive," I said to Bill, wishing I could have slipped by unseen.

He shrugged.

"Well, it's worth a try," I insisted, hurrying back to the house. There, I lathered the hideous wound with the medicine and asked myself, Why hadn't nature taken this pitiful creature right away? Why am I doing this? Life with only one wing? Poor little thing. Certain it was suffering, convinced it would die, I closed the lid. We'd done everything we could.

The next morning, we heard a stirring in the box. "Olive's eating!" said Jaymee who'd been up since daybreak, "and she's a girl."

"How can you tell?" Becky asked.

"Boys have blue and purple feathers on their heads. Olive's just plain gray—and sometimes pink when the sun shines on her."

We put the little bird in a large wire-mesh cage prepared with seeds, leaves and twigs. In the sudden shock of light and space, Olive sensed freedom and tried again to fly. She flapped her wing, repeatedly hurling herself against the wire-mesh squares, waffling her breast feathers, and falling over backward. It hurt to watch her try.

In time the wing fluttered slower and slower till finally it stopped altogether. From then on, Olive wandered around the cage sort of off-kilter, like half-a-bird, barely existing, yet taking the time to preen and rearrange her feathers as though trying to draw a cape over the gaping hole. When evenings came she curled her pink claws around a small manzanita limb we'd wedged in the bottom in one corner. There she perched in a trance-like state, dreaming of life in the sky, I supposed, a life put on hold.

Olive had been with us for a month when the egg appeared. Like an elliptical, oversized pearl, it rolled around like a magic thing between a few twigs and leaves in her favorite corner of the cage.

"Just like in the wild," Bill said, "too lazy to build a decent nest. They either lay their eggs in other birds' nests or slap three twigs together and call it home."

He was right. Doves' nests—flimsy little platforms tossed at random among the mesquite and manzanita bushes—spanned weak boughs or remnant nests of other birds. Some were precariously balanced on knots of mistletoe. Most were within easy reach of predators; the bobcat, raccoon and coyote. I'd walked often beneath branches to view the eggs from below, or discovered the empty, broken shells at my feet after they'd fallen through. Yet these birds kept right on laying in the same miserable nests time and again.

Now, here was Olive, caged, piteously wounded, soon laying an egg almost every day. For Jaymee, this was magic. But as "grown-ups," we questioned the little bird's efforts. Why was this happening? Without a mate, the eggs would be infertile. But Jaymee was a child and children make plans. Instead of worrying about why, she accepted the miracle with her whole heart—and began collecting the eggs in a tea cup.

At first Bill didn't pay much attention to the dove. He had cattle, horses and fields to care for but one Sunday, when he noticed Jaymee's cup was full, he built a wooden egg-box, a "treasure chest" with a padlock and key, and a transparent lid revealing forty two-inch cubicles padded with black velvet inside. "A safe nest for each egg," he told her. "They'll keep forever." She hugged him ecstatically. "Thank you, Daddy."

By now Olive was becoming very tame. No longer spooked by human hands, she tottered around the cage with anticipation. At the sight of Jaymee, she cooed softly, pecked seeds from her palm, ate apples, chicken mash, bacon and ice-cream. Surely, this is a sign of intelligence, I thought.

Like all creatures wild and tame, Olive responded with growing trust, and looked forward to her daily dust bath in the metal cake pan we put in her cage. She especially enjoyed her shower, a gentle misting of water from a spray bottle, after which she cleaned her feathers vigorously. We hoped she didn't hurt. We prayed she was happy. But our crippled dove's longing for her own kind showed when we moved her cage to the glassed in porch where she could look out at the cobalt sky and sun-drenched fields of green alfalfa. Occasionally, another dove would sail by and Olive's wing would quiver and her little gray head would bob anxiously, begging to be noticed.

Incredibly, the egg laying continued. Sixteen! Seventeen! Eighteen! How much longer can this go on? I wondered.

Bill shared our concern with a gruff, "She's gonna lay herself to death." At least he didn't say "dumb," I thought, and recently I'd caught him putting small logs in the cattle troughs. "Rafts," he'd said when I inquired, "so the doves can climb out when they fall in." Was he starting to care just a little bit, I wondered, or had he always...in his own way?

When the nineteenth egg arrived, so did the first storm out of Mexico. Fearsome winds and stinging sands ripped birds' nests from the trees, dashing eggs and the newly hatched to the ground. The girls spent the morning burying dead newborns before the barn cats got them, and Jaymee gathered varieties of wild bird eggs, miraculously unbroken, and put them in her treasure chest. Most had tinted shells, rainbow colors, I thought—displayed like precious jewels among pearls on velvet black.

One storm often follows another in Arizona, so I wasn't surprised when the second roared through and Jaymee dashed into the kitchen cupping a naked-pink, open-beaked, baby bird, in her hands. "It's hungry!" she cried. "Maybe Olive can be its mama."

I wasn't so sure, but Jaymee hurriedly named the newborn "Pinky." With an eye dropper we squeezed chick-mash mixed with warm water into the orphan's yawning yellow mouth, and debated bestowing such a helpless gift on our fragile dove.

What will she do? I wondered. Then I realized, what did it matter? We didn't know how to keep the hours-old creature the "right temperature" at night anyway. Only a mother bird could do that. My broody-hen hatched and raised baby ducks, guinea hens, pheasants, and quail along with her own chicks. So why couldn't a dove raise a stranger too? Besides, if it worked, life in a cage wouldn't be so lonesome for Olive.

I asked Bill what he thought. "She'll probably think he's dinner," he said.

Jaymee's eyes widened. "Oh, Daddy," she scolded. "Olive's smarter than that! We've got to try!"

"We'll fix up a nice nest first," I said, "a good sturdy one like a dove *should* make, soft and deep so the baby won't fall out." The girls found a storm damaged nest and lined it with horse hair and plenty of chicken feathers for added softness. I worried the feathers might have an alien scent Olive wouldn't appreciate but since doves frequently feasted side by side with my chickens I decided she wouldn't mind. Also, since Pinky was already a scented bouquet of human hands and chicken mash, and Olive was accustomed to both, we laid the newborn in the nest with one egg at his side. "Maybe that will help her think the baby is really hers," Jaymee said, and placed the nest inside the cage.

During the night I awoke to strange sounds, living reminders that wild birds belong outdoors—not in my kitchen. Expecting the worst, I reached for my flashlight and hurried to the scene. The nest was destroyed. At first I couldn't see any birds at all. Then, in that favorite corner where eggs were laid, one of nature's miracles unfolded like a bud in the beam of my light. On three small twigs, her bright eyes aglow with joy, nested Olive—with Pinky cradled under her wing.

The egg-laying ceased. Pinky had a mother. Proud and protective, Olive chirped anxiously when we took him out for feeding many times a day. When we put him back in "her" nest, with a little dry grass tucked around and under him so he wouldn't tip over, she paced back and forth till certain he wasn't leaving again. Then she examined him thoroughly, picking and tweaking him as though trying to weave their lives together. She loved him.

Pinky thrived. Pink skin one day. Milkweed down the next. Finally, feathers appeared on stubby wings, then everywhere. A delicate tapestry of silver-white and black, the fledgling soon needed a far more fitting name. When the short, hooked beak was topped by a tiny black-bandit mask, our bird book dubbed him a Loggerhead shrike, a lover of wetlands and rarely seen on our ranch after several years of drought. Jaymee named him "Bandit."

Bandit soon perched on Jaymee's finger like his mama. Teetering on tiny black claws, he gobbled down spaghetti, bologna and pepperoni sliced into slender worm-like strips. As more feathers grew, his gourmet palate expanded to include moths, bugs and any insect Jaymee could pick up with my eyebrow tweezers. His passion was flies, but they had to be alive.

Flies were a part of ranch and farm life, and a door rarely opened without a herd of these miserable pests stampeding in. Unable to get out, they'd sizzle up and down window panes and fell on the sills, exhausted. Then Jaymee grabbed them by one leg with the tweezers, and fed them still buzzing to Bandit, while Olive waited patiently for her serving on the bottom of the cage.

The morning we'd been dreading came when Bandit discovered that he had wings. We found him clinging upside-down to the top of the cage. Unable to figure out how to let go, he chattered, and fluttered his wings eagerly, while Olive cringed in her corner, feathers frazzled. "You're going to have to let him go," I told Jaymee.

"But he needs some practice first," she argued, removing him from the cage and perching him on her finger. Instantly, Bandit took a test flight. He shot up and positioned himself on the wagon wheel chandelier, took stock of his surroundings and shuttled awkwardly to the bullhorn hat rack, from there to the toaster. By now Olive was chirping with alarm.

"Honey. We've got to put him outside," I said.

"But the cats'll get him."

"He has to learn," I responded. Outside I put him on a cottonwood branch so he could practice flying. We watched him flit from branch to branch, and grabbed him twice when he landed on the ground. He learned fast. Too fast. The moment we tried to step inside he zipped in through the doorway and greeted us from the chandelier. Then he heard Olive and dived to the top of the cage where she watched him from below, her wing vibrating piteously.

"She wants to go with him," Jaymee said sadly.

And he doesn't understand why she doesn't come, I thought.

Bandit was housebound. Every time we took him outside he'd perch for an hour on the milk separator right by the front door, mask cocked, wings open, waiting patiently for someone to go through the door so he could sneak back in.

Night came. We knew he'd never survive with so many barn cats on the prowl. Furthermore, spring rains had lured many birds back to the lands by the White River Draw. Perhaps the shrikes would return? Until he was ready to go we had to keep him safe, so we rigged up a temporary night time cage near Olive's. She seemed pleased.

Bandit grew increasingly adept at flying and was soon darting in and out of the front door at will, eager to remain part of the only home he knew. I warned Bill and everybody else, "Be careful when you come in for lunch. Our little shrike is going to sneak in, and he might get hurt if the door shuts too quickly."

As fate would have it, Bill forgot. Worse still, it was he who had put the heavy-duty spring on the door so it would snap shut faster and not let so many flies into the house. When he saw the little bird spiral over his head and land on the rug at his feet, his first words were, "I guess I had other things on my mind besides holding a door open for a bird." But he dropped his voice. "I never saw the poor thing at all till it was lying in front of me."

For the second time that year I watched him lean over to pick up a wounded bird. Birds are so delicate and I knew he felt badly. Bandit was gasping, but the tiny needle-clawed feet gripped his calloused palm. Reassured, Bill said, "Maybe he just got the wind knocked out of him." He handed the stunned creature to me to put back in its cage...right beside Olive.

The next day, Bandit seemed cheerful enough but ruffled at being caged. We let him out. No longer the wing-testing, house-crashing maniac of previous flights, he flitted quite professionally between barn roofs, scattered trees and barbed wire fences. The little shrike had grown up and gradually he flew farther away. Easy to spot in his flashing white and black and silver, wing beats too fast to count, we watched him leave for the river.

Later in the summer, the girls were getting their projects ready for the Cochise County Fair only ten days away. Becky planned to show her horse and Jaymee busied herself grooming her rabbits for the 4-H competitions. The egg chest had been set aside perhaps for the following year when suddenly Jaymee said, "Maybe I should show Olive and her eggs in the wildlife division, too."

"But Olive's been sick," I reminded her. Indeed, after Bandit's departure the little mourning dove had begun sleeping most of the day. Eyes half closed, she perched unnaturally fluffed on her manzanita limb. The only sign she showed of interest in life came with the early dawn; a plaintive "Oooh-ah-hoo-hoo-hoo," like the sorrowful cry of a lost soul in the desert, seeking comfort. Then she started molting.

Clearly unwell, she soon didn't seem to care where she roosted, often simply crouching uncomfortably over a few stray twigs and leaves. When she stopped taking dust baths altogether and dripped resentfully in a pool of water after misting, I was afraid she was going to die. We purchased a recommended diet fortified with vitamins and antibiotics for indisposed canaries. Then we added sugar to her water and a night-light to her cage to help cheer her through the long dark hours of depression. Amazingly, she perked up.

Becky, however, weighed Jaymee's idea with an egg count. "You only have thirty-one eggs, Jaymee. That leaves nine empty holes so the project isn't complete. You'll have to wait till next year when birds start laying again."

I felt a strange sense of relief because Olive had never fully recovered from her depression despite the vitamins. She'd become frail, dusty looking, almost spectral. Around strange animals and surroundings at the fair I feared she would pick up an infection. At home she'd be safe. But the following morning she laid another egg.

We were amazed, but Bill was stunned. "Honey," he said to Jaymee. "That's one smart bird!"

A secret smile lit Jaymee's eyes. She put the egg in nest number thirty-two. "Only eight more to go," she murmured, and dashed off to catch every live fly she could find for Olive.

During the short week that followed, Olive rallied with six more eggs. Then, three days before the fair, and two more eggs to go, our weary little dove huddled on her manzanita limb for the last time. We found her in the morning, dead, like a tiny piece of driftwood washed up on desert sands.

*Love on the Wild Side*

It was sad to see Jaymee wrap Olive in one of Bill's handkerchiefs and bury her in a sunny place, "because she liked to look at the sky," she said. Then gathering two small handfuls of pale feathers from the cage, "that look more pink than gray," she filled the empty velvet nests, and locked the box forever. "I'm going to show my egg collection anyway," she told Becky.

It would be twenty years—after the blue ribbon—before we learned the truth about the tiny life we thought was "put on hold." Modern studies show that doves, unlike most birds that lay only a few eggs, will keep right on laying as long as the eggs are taken away; slip through flimsy nests, are stolen by predators—or "collected" by a little girl.

Furthermore, a dove can lay more than one clutch at a time in the wild, and incubate a second and even a third while raising a lucky survivor from the first. No wonder we have so many doves?

Today, when rainbows shimmer from the stained-glass sun-catchers Bill hangs on our window panes to protect the birds against broken necks, I remember Olive, a pale-pink mourning dove, who showed "us grown-ups" that lots of things happen if we *listen* to our children. How else could the smartest bird on earth have had the chance to show us she could raise one baby shrike, attempt to lay an entire migration, and almost fill a little girl's treasure chest?

Listen to your children, Mommy and Daddy. Make time for magic, miracles and love.

# To a Little Girl

Little girl, just half-past three,
Take this little rhyme from me,
All the joy that gold can bring,
All the songs that birds can sing,
All this world can hold to give
Grown-up men the while they live,
Hath not half the charm of you
And the lovely things you do.

Little girl, just half-past three,
Lost are dreams that used to be.
Now the things I thought worthwhile
Could not buy your lovely smile,
And I would not give you up
For the golden plate and cup
And the crown a king may boast.
In my life you're uppermost.

Little girl, just half-past three,
This is what you mean to me,
More than all that money buys,
More than any selfish prize,
More than fortune, more than fame,
And I learned this when you came.
Other fathers know it, too.
Nothing matters more than you.

—*Edgar Guest*

**TEACH Services, Inc.**
P U B L I S H I N G
www.TEACHServices.com • (800) 367-1844

We invite you to view the complete
selection of titles we publish at:
**www.TEACHServices.com**

We encourage you to write us
with your thoughts about this,
or any other book we publish at:
**info@TEACHServices.com**

TEACH Services' titles may be purchased in
bulk quantities for educational, fund-raising,
business, or promotional use.
**bulksales@TEACHServices.com**

Finally, if you are interested in seeing
your own book in print, please contact us at:
**publishing@TEACHServices.com**

We are happy to review your manuscript at no charge.

www.ingramcontent.com/pod-product-compliance
Lightning Source LLC
Chambersburg PA
CBHW020359170426
43200CB00005B/226